From **THE STORY**

"What had I to look
pect had I of being a
the cripple who painte
ple always thought it was
that I could paint with my toes
I was lucky, yes, quite a remarkable
But what difference did painting with my
left foot make? What good was it saving I
was remarkable
able—I only wa
everyone else.

"Then suddenly c
always been fond of writing letters, but now
I decided to try something more ambitious,
not just letters, but stories. The idea grew
and grew till it invaded my whole mind."

THE STORY OF CHRISTY BROWN
was originally published by
Simon and Schuster as *My Left Foot*.

THE STORY OF
CHRISTY
BROWN

by CHRISTY BROWN
(Original British title: *My Left Foot*)

With a forward and epilogue by
Dr. Robert Collis

PUBLISHED BY POCKET BOOKS NEW YORK

THE STORY OF CHRISTY BROWN

Simon and Schuster edition (titled: *My Left Foot*) published April, 1955

POCKET BOOK edition published September, 1971

Standard Book Number: 671-77349-6.
Library of Congress Catalog Card Number: 55-5951.
Copyright, ©, 1954, 1955, by Christy Brown. All rights reserved.
This POCKET BOOK edition is published by arrangement with Simon &
Schuster, Inc. This book was originally published in 1954 in Great
Britain by Martin Secker & Warburg, Ltd., under the title *My Left Foot*.
Printed in the U.S.A.

Contents

Foreword

MANY YEARS AGO *some kind theater people gave a matinee movie performance for children, under the auspices of a charitable foundation which had been formed after the second production of my play,* Marrowbone Lane. *At the end, as the children were streaming out, I saw a strange-looking little boy perched on the shoulders of a much bigger and stronger boy. They presented a most amazing spectacle, so that I can still see the picture clearly. The horse was broad-shouldered, had tousled dark hair, and his lips were twisted in a funny smile of confidence, strength, and friendliness. The rider's legs were twisted round him, his arms and hands held stiff in an odd way. What has remained most clearly in my mind, however, is the pale young face and the eyes that seemed to shine out with vitality from it. Although he is now a man of twenty-one, I can still see the same rare spiritual quality in his gaze. I asked who the boy was and was told that he was called Christy Brown and that he had been almost completely paralyzed from birth but was, apparently, quite intelligent, though he could not speak. Years passed, but I never forgot that momentary glimpse, and when four years ago, at the promptings of my sister-in-law, Eirene Collis, I set up a clinic in Dublin for the new treatment of cerebral palsy, which she had introduced into Europe from America, I thought of him at once and sought him out. After a search I found where he lived amidst a vast suburb of new workmen's houses. I knocked. A short, stoutish, round-faced, smiling woman in her forties opened the door and led me into the kitchen-living room which was filled to overflowing with numberless children of all ages, or so it seemed to me. In a big chair by the fire, propped up, sat the crippled boy I had come to seek. As I looked at him I felt an immediate impact. The other people in the room seemed to recede and I appeared to be standing alone in the presence of a personage whom I seemed to know already. He was quite unable to speak or communicate to me with his mouth, but this in no way prevented me from getting in touch with him.*

Much has passed between us in the intervening years, much which has now enabled me to write this preface.

I will not here anticipate the story which he tells so well of how he commenced his treatment for cerebral palsy, or how he learned to write, but if the reader needs certain questions answered when he has finished reading Christy's account of his progress in these respects, particularly the more medical details regarding his complaint, cerebral palsy, he can look at the epilogue which will give him these answers.

In a sense, I suppose I may claim to have taught him to write or, better, how not to write. He certainly is the best student I have ever had. This work, however, is in no way mine. True, we have planned and discussed it all the way through, true, I have been a ruthless critic, coming as I do of a strange literary family. Both my brothers are well-known writers (John Stewart, my twin, and Maurice Collis, my elder brother), and my own knowledge of writing is largely due to the advice they gave their low-brow brother. This advice, and some more which I had learned about writing myself, I gave to Christy. Not being able to talk at all well at this time, he couldn't answer back. It was therefore with immense surprise and delight that I discovered, when he started to rewrite, that he had understood everything I had said. Indeed, he had more than comprehended in the ordinary way, for, sitting alone, cut off in his little room, he had "thought it out" so that now he commenced to write with a simple style of his own, becoming quite a craftsman in a very short time. His writing has a hard, unsentimental quality due to the discipline which he has had to establish over his emotions. Also, his

*mind shows a remarkable selective quality so that the
reader is never bored, but is carried along effortlessly.*

*The picture of his extraordinary family of fourteen, as
portrayed in his narrative, is exactly as I see them. Were
you to come to Stannoway Road in Dublin you would
find there Mr. and Mrs. Brown, together with Paddy and
Peggy and Mona and Francis and Sean and Eamonn and
all the others, exactly as you had pictured them. And I
believe also you would find Christy himself as you had
hoped to find him. You would not be disappointed as you
have been when you met most of the authors you have
wanted to meet before because you had read their work.
The Browns, with their inimitable mother, are without
doubt the most remarkable family I have ever met, and I
find no greater pleasure at the end of a long day than to
go round to their house, have a crack with them all in the
kitchen, and then pass into Christy's little sanctum in
the yard and sit with him, talking or reading. Of course, the
whole thing is not quite so unusual in Ireland as it might
be elsewhere. For here one is used to having sudden angry
arguments on the merits of Ibsen with the postman, or
finding that the driver who takes the bus up 1,000 feet
to our village in the mountains is about to produce one
of the Abbey Theater plays at the local drama festival.
And one is asked continuously if one would mind "having
a little look" at the play written by the policeman on point
duty outside the hospital, or a novel by one of one's
students.*

*Apart from any literary value, and the surpassing in-
terest that Christy Brown's portrait of a Dublin family
gives us, this work seems to me of universal importance.
Seldom, except in the great story of Helen Keller and
Annie Sullivan, has a crippled, blind, or deaf person been
so gifted that he was able to lift the curtain that hangs
around the lives of so many of our less fortunate brothers
and sisters and let us see within. Never, I think, has one
read an account of a life so completely different from the
normal which has been written with such craftsmanship
that one can actually feel what the writer felt himself. For
me the whole experience has been an extraordinary revela-*

tion, and a proof of the amazing power of the spirit of man to overcome the impossible and, perhaps most of all, of the utmost need of the human soul to escape from every sort of prison.

ROBERT COLLIS

Bo-Island
Newtownmountkennedy.
March, 1954

1

THE LETTER "A"

I WAS BORN in the Rotunda Hospital, on June 5th, 1932. There were nine children before me and twelve after me, so I myself belong to the middle group. Out of this total of twenty-two, seventeen lived, but four died in infancy, leaving thirteen still to hold the family fort.

Mine was a difficult birth, I am told. Both mother and son almost died. A whole army of relations queued up outside the hospital until the small hours of the morning, waiting for news and praying furiously that it would be good.

After my birth mother was sent to recuperate for some weeks and I was kept in the hospital while she was away. I remained there for some time, without name, for I wasn't baptized until my mother was well enough to bring me to church.

It was mother who first saw that there was something wrong with me. I was about four months old at the time. She noticed that my head had a habit of falling backward whenever she tried to feed me. She attempted to correct this by placing her hand on the back of my neck to keep it steady. But when she took it away, back it would drop again. That was the first warning sign. Then she became aware of other defects as I got older. She saw that my hands were clenched nearly all of the time and were inclined to twine behind my back, my mouth couldn't grasp the teat of the bottle because even at that early age my jaws would either lock together tightly, so that it was impossible for her to open them, or they would suddenly become limp and fall loose, dragging my whole mouth to one side. At six months I could not sit up without having a mountain of pillows around me. At twelve months it was the same.

Very worried by this, mother told my father her fears, and they decided to seek medical advice without any further delay. I was a little over a year old when they began to take me to hospitals and clinics, convinced that there was something definitely wrong with me, something which they could not understand or name, but which was very real and disturbing.

Almost every doctor who saw and examined me, labeled me a very interesting but also a hopeless case. Many told mother very gently that I was mentally defective and would remain so. That was a hard blow to a young mother who had already reared five healthy children. The doctors were so very sure of themselves that mother's faith in me seemed almost an impertinence. They assured her that nothing could be done for me.

She refused to accept this truth, the inevitable truth—as it then seemed—that I was beyond cure, beyond saving, even beyond hope. She could not and would not believe that I was an imbecile, as the doctors told her. She had nothing in the world to go by, not a scrap of evidence to support her conviction that, though my body was crippled, my mind was not. In spite of all the doctors and specialists told her, she would not agree. I don't believe she knew why—she just knew, without feeling the smallest shade of doubt.

Finding that the doctors could not help in any way beyond telling her not to place her trust in me, or, in other words, to forget I was a human creature, rather to regard me as just something to be fed and washed and then put away again, mother decided there and then to take matters into her own hands. I was *her* child, and therefore part of the family. No matter how dull and incapable I might grow up to be, she was determined to treat me on the same plane as the others, and not as the "queer one" in the back room who was never spoken of when there were visitors present.

That was a momentous decision as far as my future life was concerned. It meant that I would always have my mother on my side to help me fight all the battles that were to come, and to inspire me with new strength when I was almost beaten. But it wasn't easy for her because now the relatives and friends had decided otherwise. They contended that I should be taken kindly, sympathetically, but not seriously. That would be a mistake. "For your own sake," they told her, "don't look to this boy as you would to the others; it would only break your heart in the end." Luckily for me, mother and father held out against the lot of them. But mother wasn't content just to say that I was not an idiot: she set out to prove it, not because of any rigid sense of duty, but out of love. That is why she was so successful.

At this time she had the five other children to look after besides the "difficult one," though as yet it was not by any means a full house. They were my brothers, Jim, Tony, and Paddy, and my two sisters, Lily and Mona, all of them very young, just a year or so between each of them, so that they were almost exactly like steps of stairs.

Four years rolled by and I was now five, and still as helpless as a newly born baby. While my father was out at bricklaying, earning our bread and butter for us, mother was slowly, patiently pulling down the wall, brick by brick, that seemed to thrust itself between me and the other children, slowly, patiently penetrating beyond the thick curtain that hung over my mind, separating it from theirs. It was hard, heartbreaking work, for often all she got from me in return was a vague smile and perhaps a faint gurgle. I could not speak or even mumble, nor could I sit up without support on my own, let alone take steps. But I wasn't inert or motionless. I seemed, indeed, to be convulsed with movement, wild, stiff, snakelike movement that never left me, except in sleep. My fingers twisted and twitched continually, my arms twined backwards and would often shoot out suddenly this way and that, and my head lolled and sagged sideways. I was a queer, crooked little fellow.

Mother tells me how one day she had been sitting with me for hours in an upstairs room, showing me pictures out of a great big storybook that I had got from Santa

Claus last Christmas and telling me the names of the different animals and flowers that were in them, trying without success to get me to repeat them. This had gone on for hours while she talked and laughed with me. Then at the end of it she leaned over me and said gently into my ear:

"Did you like it, Chris? Did you like the bears and the monkeys and all the lovely flowers? Nod your head for yes, like a good boy."

But I could make no sign that I had understood her. Her face was bent over mine hopefully. Suddenly, involuntarily, my queer hand reached up and grasped one of the dark curls that fell in a thick cluster about her neck. Gently she loosened the clenched fingers, though some dark strands were still clutched between them.

Then she turned away from my curious stare and left the room, crying. The door closed behind her. It all seemed hopeless. It looked as though there was some justification for my relatives' contention that I was an idiot and beyond help.

They now spoke of an institution.

"Never!" said my mother almost fiercely, when this was suggested to her. "I know my boy is not an idiot. It is his body that is shattered, not his mind. I'm sure of that."

Sure? Yet inwardly, she prayed God would give her some proof of her faith. She knew it was one thing to believe but quite another thing to prove.

I was now five, and still I showed no real sign of intelligence. I showed no apparent interest in things except with my toes—more especially those of my left foot. Although my natural habits were clean, I could not aid myself, but in this respect my father took care of me. I used to lie on my back all the time in the kitchen or, on bright warm days, out in the garden, a little bundle of crooked muscles and twisted nerves, surrounded by a family that loved me and hoped for me and that made me part of their own warmth and humanity. I was lonely, imprisoned in a world of my own, unable to communicate with others, cut off, separated from them as though a glass wall stood between my existence and theirs, thrusting me beyond the sphere of their lives and activities. I longed to run about and play with the rest, but I was unable to break loose from my bondage.

Then, suddenly, it happened! In a moment everything was changed, my future life molded into a definite shape, my mother's faith in me rewarded and her secret fear changed into open triumph.

It happened so quickly, so simply after all the years of waiting and uncertainty, that I can see and feel the whole scene as if it had happened last week. It was the afternoon of a cold, gray December day. The streets outside glistened with snow, the white sparkling flakes stuck and melted on the windowpanes and hung on the boughs of the trees like molten silver. The wind howled dismally, whipping up little whirling columns of snow that rose and fell at every fresh gust. And over all, the dull, murky sky stretched like a dark canopy, a vast infinity of grayness.

Inside, all the family were gathered round the big kitchen fire that lit up the little room with a warm glow and made giant shadows dance on the walls and ceiling.

In a corner Mona and Paddy were sitting, huddled together, a few torn school primers before them. They were writing down little sums on to an old chipped slate, using a bright piece of yellow chalk. I was close to them, propped up by a few pillows against the wall, watching.

It was the chalk that attracted me so much. It was a long, slender stick of vivid yellow. I had never seen anything like it before, and it showed up so well against the black surface of the slate that I was fascinated by it as much as if it had been a stick of gold.

Suddenly, I wanted desperately to do what my sister was doing. Then—without thinking or knowing exactly what I was doing, I reached out and took the stick of chalk out of my sister's hand—with my left foot.

I do not know why I used my left foot to do this. It is a puzzle to many people as well as to myself, for, although I had displayed a curious interest in my toes at an early age, I had never attempted before this to use either of my feet in any way. They could have been as useless to me as were my hands. That day, however, my left foot, apparently by its own volition, reached out and very impolitely took the chalk out of my sister's hand.

I held it tightly between my toes, and, acting on an impulse, made a wild sort of scribble with it on the slate. Next moment I stopped, a bit dazed, surprised, looking down at the stick of yellow chalk stuck between my toes, not knowing what to do with it next, hardly knowing how it got there. Then I looked up and became aware that everyone had stopped talking and was staring at me silently. Nobody stirred. Mona, her black curls framing her chubby little face, stared at me with great big eyes and open mouth. Across the open hearth, his face lit by flames, sat my father, leaning forward, hands outspread on his knees, his shoulders tense. I felt the sweat break out on my forehead.

My mother came in from the pantry with a steaming pot in her hand. She stopped midway between the table and the fire, feeling the tension flowing through the room. She followed their stare and saw me in the corner. Her eyes looked from my face down to my foot, with the chalk gripped between my toes. She put down the pot.

Then she crossed over to me and knelt down beside me, as she had done so many times before.

"I'll show you what to do with it, Chris," she said, very slowly and in a queer, choked way, her face flushed as if with some inner excitement.

Taking another piece of chalk from Mona, she hesitated, then very deliberately drew, on the floor in front of me, *the single letter "A."*

"Copy that," she said, looking steadily at me. "Copy it, Christy."

I couldn't.

I looked about me, looked around at the faces that were turned towards me, tense, excited faces that were at that moment frozen, immobile, eager, waiting for a miracle in their midst.

The stillness was profound. The room was full of flame and shadow that danced before my eyes and lulled my taut nerves into a sort of waking sleep. I could hear the sound of the water tap dripping in the pantry, the loud ticking of the clock on the mantelshelf, and the soft hiss and crackle of the logs on the open hearth.

I tried again. I put out my foot and made a wild jerking stab with the chalk which produced a very crooked line and nothing more. Mother held the slate steady for me.

"Try again, Chris," she whispered in my ear. "Again."

I did. I stiffened my body and put my left foot out again, for the third time. I drew one side of the letter. I drew half the other side. Then the stick of chalk broke and I was left with a stump. I wanted to fling it away and give up. Then I felt my mother's hand on my shoulder. I tried once more. Out went my foot. I shook, I sweated and strained every muscle. My hands were so tightly clenched that my fingernails bit into the flesh. I set my teeth so hard that I nearly pierced my lower lip. Everything in the room swam till the faces around me were mere patches of white. But—I drew it—*the letter "A."* There it was on the floor before me. Shaky, with awkward, wobbly sides and a very uneven center line. But it *was* the letter "A." I looked up. I saw my mother's face for a moment, tears on her cheeks. Then my father stooped and hoisted me on to his shoulder.

I had done it! It had started—the thing that was to give my mind its chance of expressing itself. True, I couldn't speak with my lips. But now I would speak through something more lasting than spoken words—written words.

That one letter, scrawled on the floor with a broken bit of yellow chalk gripped between my toes, was my road to a new world, my key to mental freedom. It was to provide a source of relaxation to the tense, taut thing that was I, which panted for expression behind a twisted mouth.

2

M-O-T-H-E-R

HAVING TAUGHT ME to draw the letter "A" with my foot, mother next set out to teach me the whole alphabet in much the same way. She was determined to make use of the opportunity so miraculously presented to her and to help me communicate with the rest through the written word, if not through the spoken one.

My memory of the way she set about this is quite clear. She would bring me up into the front bedroom any day she wasn't too busy with the household, and spend hours teaching me one letter after the other. She would write down each letter on the floor with a piece of chalk. Then she would rub them out with a duster and make me write them down again from memory with the chalk held between my toes. It was hard work for both of us. Often she would be in the pantry cooking the dinner when I'd give a howl to make her come up to see if I had spelled a word correctly. If I was wrong, I'd make her kneel down, her hands covered with flour, and show me the right way to do it. I remember the first thing I learned to write was my initials: "C. B.," though I'd often become confused and put the "B" before the "C." Whenever anyone asked me what my name was, I'd grab a piece of chalk and write "C. B." with a great flourish.

Soon afterwards I learned to write my full name instead of just two initials. I was tremendously proud of myself when I could do this. I felt quite important.

I was now going on six, and soon I got tired of just writing my own name. I wanted to do something else—something bigger. But I couldn't, because I couldn't read. I didn't exactly know what being able to read meant. I just knew that Jim could do it, Tony could do it, that Mona and Peter could do it, and that made me want to do it too. I think I was jealous.

Slowly, very painfully, I ploughed through the whole twenty-six letters with my mother and gradually mastered each of them in turn. One thing that gave mother great encouragement at this time was my ability to listen and watch attentively when she was sitting by my side giving me lessons. My attention seldom wavered.

I remember us sitting in the big horsehair armchair before a big fire one winter's evening. The baby was asleep in the pram on the other side of the hearthstone. The two of us were alone in the dim-lit kitchen, while my father was at a bricklayers' meeting and my sisters and brothers were out playing on the streets. My mother had Peter's schoolbook in her hand and she was reading little stories about the poor children of Lir who were turned into swans by their wicked stepmother, about Diarmud and Graine and the King who turned everything he touched into gold. She read on to me till the shadows had made the room dark and little Eamonn stirred and cried in his sleep. Then she got up and switched on the lights. The spell broke and the enchantment was gone.

Knowing the alphabet was half the battle won, for I was soon able to put letters together and to form little words. After a while I began to know how to put words together and form sentences. I was getting on. But it wasn't as easy or as simple as it sounds. Mother had by now seven other children to care for besides myself. Fortunately she had a real ally in my sister Lily, or "Titch," as the others nicknamed her. She was the eldest and the little mother of the circle, a small, wiry kid with flowing black curls and flashing eyes. She could be very sweet when she liked—quite a proper little angel. But she wasn't very angelic when she was roused. She realized my mother's tough situation quicker than any grown woman would, and responded. She busied herself looking after the others so that mother could spend more time with me. She cooked, and washed and dressed the smaller ones, and made sure the bigger ones washed behind their ears every morning before setting out for school. Perhaps she was just a shade too zealous, for often Jim or Tony would slink, shamefaced, into the kitchen, bearing testimony to little Lily's earnest housewifery in the form of swollen ears or black eyes.

I could still not speak intelligibly, but by now I had a sort of grunting language which the family understood more or less.

Whenever I got into difficulties and they couldn't make out what I was saying, I'd point to the floor and print the words out on it with my left foot. If I couldn't spell the words I wanted to write, I flew into a rage, which only made me grunt still more incoherently.

Although I couldn't talk very much at seven years old, I was now able to sit up alone and crawl about from place to place on my bottom without breaking any bones or smashing any of mother's china. I wore no shoes or any other kind of footwear. My mother had tried to make me used to having my feet covered from an early age, saying I looked very much neglected barefooted. But whenever she put anything on my feet I always kicked it off again quickly. I hated having my feet covered. When mother put shoes or stockings on my feet, I felt as any normal person might feel if his hands were tied behind his back.

As time went on, I began to depend more and more on my left foot for everything. It was my main means of communication, of making myself understood to the family. Very slowly it became indispensable to me. With it I learned to break down some of the barriers that stood between me and the others at home. It was the only key to the door of the prison I was in.

It was my habit when I had written something down on the floor, to spit on it, rub it out with my heel, and then to write it down again from memory as I did when mother was teaching me. One day when I was about six and a half a local doctor came to visit my brother who had sprained his wrist while playing a game of rugger. After coming downstairs, the doctor saw me writing on the floor with some chalk between my toes. He was incredulous. He began to ask mother questions about me and, being anxious to show him that I understood all that was being said, she put me up on the table and invited him to ask me to write something for him. He thought for a moment, then he took out his big report ledger from his bag, offered me a big red pencil and asked me to write my name in the book.

I took the pencil between my toes, pulled the book towards me, steadied myself, and slowly wrote my name on the flyleaf in big block-letter capitals.

"Amazing! I'm astonished, Mrs. Brown. It really is—" he began. Then he stopped in surprise, and mother blushed in confusion, for, after hesitating a bit, I had spat very deliberately on the page and was trying vigorously to erase what I had written, not understanding why the penciled letters wouldn't come off as easily as chalked ones!

The doctor brushed my mother's apologies aside with a laugh, patted me on the head and told me I was a great chap. He visited me often after that and followed my progress keenly for many years.

Meanwhile the family was multiplying steadily. The steps of stairs were mounting higher and higher. I was growing, too. My body was filling out and becoming bigger, and so was my mind. Mother found I had already passed beyond the ABC stage and almost beyond her teaching powers, too. I wasn't content any more just to sit and listen while mother read aloud to me. I was restless to be able to read myself, like Peter or Mona. I was also anxious to show them that what they could do I could do too. I began to use a pencil now instead of the chalk, although I could never get used to a pen. I once tried to write my name with my father's best fountain pen while a couple of neighbors stood round in expectation. But, to mother's embarrassment, I flung the pen away in disgust when I found it would do nothing but stick in the paper every time I tried to write with it.

My mother, knowing it was impossible to get me going to school like the others, was worried as to how she could best aid me in that way, for, although she was satisfied now that my mental state was quite normal, she feared very much that I would grow up to be illiterate and therefore at a great disadvantage intellectually as well as physically. This fear was with her almost continually. It tormented her. It wasn't because of any sense of shame at the prospect of having an illiterate, as well as a crippled, son. She thought only of the material drawback it would mean to me when I got older. She wanted above all to make me equal with my sisters and brothers in every way possible, and, as I could not go to school, she did all she could to lessen the consequences of that disadvantage herself. But she hadn't much time or chance to do this daily, for she already had her hands full, struggling to carry us all through times of unemployment, illnesses and many other worries. She found it difficult to smile at times, though somehow or other she always managed to do so.

When mother was busy, I worked on by myself, trying to make out words whenever I came across them. I used to try and spell out the names of the objects around me at home, like fire, picture, dog, door, chair, and so on. I was very proud of myself when I had mastered a new word and could write it down for mother to show her what a great scholar I was.

One day I had been trying particularly hard to master a new word that I had come upon in Peter's schoolbook. At last I got it and turned to mother, who was sitting in a chair by the fire nursing my baby brother. It was evening, the dying April light made a pattern on the floor and shone on the polished top of the little mahogany table, showing up the crack that zigzagged across its surface. Tea hadn't started yet, and all the others were upstairs playing a game of school. I sat crouched in a corner of the sofa, Peter's book before me and a pencil in my left foot. Many times that day I had looked over appealingly to where mother sat, despairing of making this word out by myself. But, seeing her rocking gently in the chair, holding the baby closely against her breast, I had turned my face away again, feeling in a vague sort of way that, somehow or other, I must work out this one word for myself without my mother's help.

A few minutes later I gave a big whoop of triumph that made mother start and the baby stir uneasily in her arms.

"What is it, Chris?" she asked me. "You'll waken the baby."

But I didn't care. In my own queer, grunting way I told her to come over to me at once.

"A new word, is it?" she said as she came across and sat down on the edge of the sofa, the baby asleep in her arms.

I grinned and, taking up the pencil, wrote down the word which had puzzled me for so long. When it was done I looked up into her face for her approval, and saw she was staring silently at what I had written on the margin of the page. She remained so still and thoughtful for so long that I became anxious and nudged her with my foot. She turned, placed her hand upon me, and smiled.

The new word which I had learned to write for the first time was—M-O-T-H-E-R.

3

"HOME"

I WAS NOW seven years old and beginning to associate with children of my own age through the help of my brothers. They took me with them when they went out to play in the streets after school, pushing me along in a rusty old go-car which they called my "chariot." Some of the best years of my life were passed in that battered old crock with the twisted handle and crooked wheels, which creaked and groaned as they raced me along in it through lamplit streets and down dark murky alleys in the bright warm twilight of a June evening or the cold grayness of a December night.

Very soon I, too, had pals with whom I had lots of fun. These were boys from our own neighborhood who were young enough and frank enough to accept me as one of themselves without asking any questions. They had grown up with me, and in a way they found it easier to associate with me than would other boys who had never seen or been with me before. Indeed, many of them regarded my affliction as some queer sort of symbol of superiority, almost of godliness, so that they treated me with deference, respect, in a strange childish way.

I had now improved so much that I could sit up in the go-car without having any pillows behind my back to support me. I took many a fall on those rides. When the car would topple over as they pushed it round a bend at full speed, I would go tumbling onto the ground amid shouts and screams. But I grew to be quite hardy in this way and became quite adept at falling in such a manner that all I ever got, even from a bad fall, was a bruising and a scrape or two. I got a huge thrill out of it all.

In our house the great thing was food. To us children mealtimes never came too soon. We'd all wait patiently till mother laid the table, then we'd make a beeline for it, I scrambling between them on my bottom and usually managing to get there first by throwing myself across a chair to show it was engaged till some of the bigger ones would lift me on to it. Then the fight began—to see which one of us would outdo the rest in eating. We cared very little about the drinking part of the proceedings. Our chief aim was to stuff ourselves with as much bread and butter as we could manage to consume without actually bursting. I couldn't feed myself, of course, but that didn't stop me from taking a very active part in those table contests. My mother or father would sit by me and feed me. Their hands often became tired from the simple process of lifting the bread and putting it into my mouth.

"Might as well be trying to fill the Liffey!" my father would complain, reaching out to the bread plate for the seventh or eighth time.

We all tried to beat the other, and every one of us gave a good account of himself, but Peter always won. When mother said, "How many?" we always all shouted together, "Three slices."

Then, after tea, if we decided not to go out, we would get together and have a game of hide-and-seek, or maybe blind-man's-buff. On such occasions father, seeing what was afoot, would immediately get up from his chair, throw his newspaper down, put on his coat and hat, and tell mother as he went out of the door, "I'll be back when they're all in bed!"

There would be the throw of a half-penny and a shout of "Heads or tails?" to decide which one of us was to be the "blind man." Someone would get an old scarf or woolen sock, tie it over the eyes of whoever had been chosen, and the game would be on. Everyone would run about the blindfolded figure, laughing while he sought blindly to catch hold of a flying arm or wriggling leg and all the time he would be buffeted around the room by friendly pats and shoves: It wasn't a very gentle game.

Sometimes the part of the "blind man" would fall to me. They'd tie a scarf around my eyes, wait a second till they had got themselves places, and then shout "ready!"

I'd pause a moment, waiting to catch the least sound of an intaken breath or a giggle that would indicate where someone was hiding, then, very cautiously, I'd crawl in the direction of the sound, pushing myself along on my behind till I had reached the spot. Then out I'd shoot my left foot, toes tensed to catch the leg of Peter's trousers or the hem of Mona's frock. When I caught someone, I'd drag them toward me and wrap my legs around them till they shouted or, more often, gasped, "I—give in!" I'd release them then, and the blindfold would be taken off my eyes and passed on to them.

Once on Hallowe'en night, when I was about eight, we brought in a few of our pals to have a little party while father and mother were out. We had the whole house to ourselves that night, and we needed it, for there was quite a crowd of us. My three sisters had brought along some of their companions as well, so that there were seven girls and about double that number of boys, all dressed up in weird costumes and fearsome masks. We made short work of the apples and nuts and all the rest. Then we played a game of hide-and-seek. I was going to be clever, for I had overheard one of the girls, a plump little creature of twelve called Sally, with red cheeks and a mass of tawny curls, tell Mona that she was going to hide in the big bath in the pantry where no one would dream of looking because they'd think it was full of water, as was usually the case. That night, however, the bath was empty, and Sally was sure she had found the ideal hiding-place.

I crawled as quickly as I could into the dark pantry before Sally got there and concealed myself right underneath the big enamel bath. There was lots of old rubbish stuck there, like old boots, clothes, stout bottles and so on, and every time I moved the end of an old umbrella would poke into my ribs. But I managed to endure it, and a few minutes later I heard someone enter the pantry and come towards the bath. I peeped out, and from the patch of light coming through the slit in the door from the kitchen inside, I saw the latter half of two thin white legs with sandals covering the feet. I knew it was Sally.

I heard her climb into the bath, but she didn't pull the lid down on herself as I thought she would, and I thought what a fool she must be, for if anyone came in she'd be easily seen, even in the dark, for she had on a white silk frock.

A few minutes later someone did come in, and from the sound of hobnailed boots on the concrete floor I knew it was one of the boys. I had been waiting for this, and it was my plan to yell out so they'd come and catch Sally before she'd time to get away. I took a breath, preparing to shout, but next moment the hobnailed boots strode across to the bath and a voice, which I recognized as that of Charlie, one of our pals, spoke in a whisper.

"Sally—are you there?" it said.

"Charlie? Yes, I'm waiting," Sally instantly replied. Then she added cautiously, "Don't make a noise."

"I won't," he said. Then he hoisted himself over the edge of the bath and dropped into it. Next I heard the lid being closed over the two of them.

I crawled out from my hiding-spot, feeling a crick in my neck, and sat at the side of the bath, listening. From within there came sounds of giggling and smothered laughter. I crawled closer and put my ear to where there was a division in the lid, leaving a space of about two inches. I could hear plainly now.

"Love me?" I heard Sally ask, followed by a giggle.

" 'Course," Charlie replied, matter-of-factly, and this in turn was followed by the sound of a very loud kiss.

I turned away in disgust, because I felt sure that Charlie was a sissy to stay with a girl rather than with the other boys. I was creeping away towards the door when I thought of something.

I smiled to myself in the dark as I crawled back to the bath and, as noiselessly as I could, lifted myself up by the side of it and leaned over as close as possible to where the two water taps were that led into the bath. I made some noise, but the two inside seemed to be too engrossed to hear it.

I couldn't use my hands, and I couldn't use my feet, either, in the position I was in. So I stretched forward more and, pressing my forehead against one of the taps, slowly twisted the handle round with my head, though it hurt me a lot. Next moment the tap was on full, with the water gushing from it into the bath.

I dropped down and made for the door, crawling as quickly as a spider. From behind I heard the lid of the bath being flung up and poor Sally screaming "Mammy! Mammy!" as she and Charlie scrambled out onto the floor. Just in time I slipped through the door and into the kitchen before either of them had got the water out of their eyes.

Neither Sally nor Charlie ever came to our house after that.

Christmas was always a jolly time with us, even if at times we hadn't much to celebrate it with. Still, no matter how little money there was in the house, Santa always came with little gifts wrapped in a lot of brightly colored paper—to make them look big and exciting. We often had to unroll sheet after sheet of paper before we'd discover the little toy that lay inside—cheap, plain little things bought in cheap, plain little shops tucked away in side streets and stuffy little corners of Dublin that no one ever had heard of before. But these presents meant more to us, lying there on our pillows on Christmas morning, than the most expensive set of trains or toy motorcars.

The night before, every one of the children would be put to bed early in the evening, except me. Mother had managed to get in a radio, paying half a crown a week for it, and every Christmas Eve I'd be let stay up to hear high mass at midnight coming from the Holy Ghost Fathers in Kimmage Manor, because I wasn't able to go to mass like the others. Mother had taught me to pray, and I could now follow mass a little when I heard it over the radio, but I didn't understand all that the priest said, especially when he spoke in that funny language which father told me was called Latin. I often asked myself what made the priest say all his prayers in Latin. Peter said it was because all the saints only spoke Latin and God couldn't understand English.

My mother tried hard to make me interested in the catechism as I got older, but it never appealed to me as much as the stories about King Lir and his swan-children. When mother told me how God made the world in seven days, I took it for granted, without asking any questions about it. But when she told me the story of Lir, I must have asked her a dozen questions about how the children were turned into swans, and why their stepmother did it, and so on. I thought it was a better story altogether. When Tony told me that God had built everything in the world, I called him a dirty liar, because I had heard father say that only bricklayers could build houses, and I knew God wasn't a bricklayer.

Tony was a wild kid. He was always getting into trouble at home and outside. He was a bit of a Romeo. He had all the girls in the neighborhood running after him, though he didn't care a rap for any of them, not even for Nancy, who was considered the belle of the place. He was the handsomest of us all, a tall, sallow-faced young fellow, very strong, very quick tempered, with curly black hair, big hands, and white teeth that flashed when he smiled or laughed. Everyone at home was a little in awe of him, and I made him my first hero.

I helped him once out of a tight fix. I was going on

eight and Tony was about thirteen. He and a pal fell out over something and they bashed each other round till Tony put his chum down for the count. Then somebody squealed about it to father and Tony was biffed very soundly and locked in the back bedroom for a week.

The next night was Hallowe'en. All the gang had saved up to buy fireworks, and everyone was going to have a good time. But my father was stern. Tony must stay at home and "learn his lesson." That was that.

Poor Tony was desperate. None of the others at home would help him.

"If I only had the blinking key!" he groaned from behind the bedroom door. But the others wouldn't listen to him.

I was mad at them. I wanted to help Tony, just to show them that *I* had some spunk. I didn't exactly know what I could do, but I knew that mother had the key in her apron pocket: I had heard father tell her to put it there as it was the safest place.

How to get it out from there was my problem.

Then I had an idea. I didn't like it. But it was the only way.

I crawled over to mother, who was sitting on the sofa sewing my father's overalls, and laid my head on her lap with a great sad sigh. She looked up, surprised, for this wasn't like me. I hated being pampered.

"What is it—tired?" she said, laying down her needle and thread. I nodded very wanly, and she stooped and lifted me up into her lap.

"We'll sing you a song to make the sandman come," she said. Then she started to sing softly some old Irish ballad that would have put anyone to sleep.

I shut my eyes and in a few minutes I was snoring very convincingly. Then, cautiously, I moved my left foot closer to mother's apron pocket, stopped, and moved it again so that this time it was actually inside the pocket. I began to explore its contents carefully. There were all sorts of odds and ends in it—scissors, buttons, and spools of thread. I was just going to give up when suddenly my toes touched something cold and steely and I knew it was the key at last. I fastened my toes around it and slowly wriggled my foot out of mother's pocket, clutching the key tightly.

I did it all so quietly and carefully that mother never suspected anything. She thought I was only moving in my sleep.

After a while she put me down gently on the sofa, throwing an old coat over me to keep me warm. Then, still humming softly to herself, she went into the pantry to get the evening dinner ready.

The moment she left the kitchen I flung the coat off me, slipped from the sofa, and crawled to the door as quickly as I could. Luckily it was open, so I got out into the hall and pulled myself up the stairs backwards like a crab and reached the landing without breaking my neck.

I kicked on the bedroom door with my left foot. My brother's voice, sounding very suspicious, spoke from within.

"Who's there?" I managed to make him understand it was I. "What do you want?" he asked me.

I grunted that I had the key. Immediately there was a scramble from inside the room, and next moment Tony and I were crouched down on each side of the door, looking at each other through the slit. We saw eye to eye for the first and last time in our lives.

"Good! Can you slide it under the door?" said Tony, speaking in a whisper. I tried to, but the slit wasn't wide enough to let the key pass through. It got stuck halfway!

"I'll make it!" said my brother grimly. Then he took his penknife from his trousers pocket and began to scrape some of the wood off the bottom of the door till it was a good half-inch wider.

"Try now!" he said to me. I pushed the key in again, and this time it slid under smoothly. "Great stuff!" he exclaimed. I heard him get up from the floor, and in a few seconds the lock was turned and Tony stepped out onto the landing, a big grin on his face.

He bent and pulled my ear. "You're a brick, Chris," he said. "Better than the lot of 'em!"

Then he ran down the stairs like a sprinter, paused at

the bottom to wave and grin back at me, and next second opened the front door noiselessly and went out.

I clambered down the stairs, crept into the kitchen, and crawled back onto the sofa while mother was still busy in the scullery, cooking the dinner. She never missed the key.

"What's happened to the door?" father asked angrily later, looking at the spot where Tony had pared it.

"Mice," said Tony, as he knelt down to say his prayers.

4

HENRY

AT EIGHT YEARS the old go-car was still my chariot, and I went about in it like any royal king. It was an ugly, battered old thing that nobody ever treated well. It was always being kicked, knocked over, shoved about, and trampled on. Everybody joked about it. But to me it was something lovable, almost human. It seemed to have some queer dignity of its own that nobody but I could appreciate. I called it Henry. I had seen my first glimpse of outdoor life sitting on its seat with the feathers sticking out of it. I can remember the wet wind on my face that day as they raced me along through busy streets. I can remember sitting in it as my brothers sat playing cards with their pals under a street lamp on a dark winter night when the gutters on the road were running with water and the lamplight was reflected in them so that they looked like little rivers of gold in the dark.

Old Henry was my throne. On it I tasted adventure and excitement with the others. They took me with them everywhere, even to the local cinema every week end. I would go in perched on the back of my big brother Jim. I noticed how the other kids would stare at me and how Jim would tell them to scram, but I didn't think about it be-

cause I didn't see why I shouldn't be perched on my
brother's back. I had always gone about on somebody's
back ever since I could remember. I didn't know why.

I liked going to the "pictures." I liked the way the lights
went out and the whole cinema grew dark before the long
slender beam of light shot over our heads from the back
and fell on to the big screen, making it alive and bright
and dazzling our eyes, and then the sudden deep hush, and
the picture would be on.

One time when we were at a movie Peter and some of
our pals tried to get me to smoke. They were experiment-
ing themselves with a packet of cigarettes that Peter had
pinched from father's pocket earlier in the day. But when
they stuck a cigarette in my mouth, I immediately began
to chew it and had the whole thing eaten before they'd
time to light it! Peter looked at me horrified, expecting me
to turn green or else start belching tobacco. But I just
grinned and opened my mouth for more. He didn't give
me any more!

Summer came. The poor little row of forget-me-nots
along the wall came out bravely, their tiny starlike blos-
soms all blue and white and speckled red. The big tree in
our neighbor's garden next door was covered with leaves
of light green, and the moss clinging to its bark looked
moist and shone with little gems of dew that sparkled in
the sunlight. Outside on the streets the flies swarmed and
buzzed over the garbage bins and flickered about the heads
of dogs sleeping on doorsteps or curled up in gardens.

It was too hot and sweaty for the cinema. So my brothers gave old Henry a spring cleaning and took me for long
"walks" out into the suburbs of Dublin, or, perhaps, on
Sundays, they'd take me up into the Phoenix Park where
we'd spend the day lying on the grass and then go down
into Donnelly's Hollow and light a fire and make tea in a
rusty old billycan while munching sandwiches and telling
stories about things that never happened, till it was shadowy and time to go home.

It was all great fun, going on these little outings. People
would sometimes stop and stare at me as my brothers

wheeled me along, but I didn't worry about it because I had no idea why they stared. Perhaps I had an idea lurking at the back of my mind that there was something wrong somewhere, something about me that made people look at me in that funny way as they passed. But it was a strange idea and it frightened me, so I tried not to think about it at all. I just wanted to be happy. And my brothers saw to it that I was happy.

I remember a little trip we took out into the country beyond Dublin one day when I was about eight and a half. We set out at about ten on a bright, warm Sunday morning in July. Old Henry had been specially oiled and polished up the night before and in consequence he was groaning a little less fiercely this morning. Peter dumped his books in the attic and stuffed his schoolbag with sandwiches and a nine-penny bottle of sauce. Two bottles of milk were pushed beneath the cushion of my car. They bruised my behind every time the go-car jolted. There were five of us, my two brothers, two pals, and myself. We all had our Sunday clothes on and Peter had dosed his head with hair oil he'd pinched from Tony. "I'm like Clark Gable now, aren't I?" he said, looking at himself before the dusty fly-marked mirror that hung on the wall above our bed. Just as he said this, a step sounded on the stairs and we heard Tony muttering to himself as he came up.

"I'm missing!" whispered Peter as he dived under the bed. Then the door opened and Tony stuck his head in.

"Seen Peter?" he asked us, glaring round the room.

"Gone to mass," answered Paddy casually as he fixed his tie.

"He pinched my Brylcreem again," growled Tony as he went down the stairs angrily.

"Is he gone?" Peter asked furtively, peeping out from beneath the bed.

"Yeah—but he'll murder you when he gets you!" warned Paddy.

"Terrible dusty under there," said Peter, brushing himself as he stood up, not caring as always.

Well, we got away at last and a few hours later were

camped on the bank of a mountain stream. I sat on the edge of the bank, fascinated as I looked down into the sun-flecked water and saw the little forms of fish flitting like shadows in and out of the waving green moss on the bottom. A bunch of these little silvery creatures gathered right below me round a slanting shelf of rock. Quickly I kicked off one of my sandals and thrust my left foot into the water, thinking I might catch one of them between my toes. But I was ignorant of fish's habits, and they darted away in a flurry of streaks and ripples to the opposite bank, well beyond the reach of my foot.

We had a fine day. Paddy became friendly with a cow from a near-by field, a big, fat, brown animal with sleepy eyes and an enormous tail that coiled about its hind legs like a rope.

"I'm going to milk it!" he told us, and we all laughed at him. But he coaxed the old cow with endearments whispered into her ear and finally got her standing still while he sat down on a tree stump, placed the billycan under her, and grinned at us. "Now watch!" he said.

We watched, but the moment he reached out and put his hand on the cow's udder, she lashed out indignantly with one of her hind legs and sent him sprawling over on to his back. Then she ambled away, her tail swishing.

"That one's a lady anyway!" said Paddy. We roared.

Towards evening we set out for home, but by the time we had got halfway, we were very hungry. Our grub had run out about two hours earlier, and we had nothing left except the empty milk bottles. Twilight was now setting in and we still had a long way to go. I wasn't so bad, for, although I was hungry, I didn't have to walk like the others: I just sat back while they took turns at pushing me along.

"I'm starving," Peter complained, his shoulders drooping.

"Shut up, so am I," growled Paddy in return, striding on.

Paddy told Peter he should have brought more sandwiches, that he must have thought they were all chickens. Peter just called him a name.

We were all losing our tempers when, suddenly, on coming round a bend in the road, we saw before us a big country house with wrought-iron gates in front and a concrete wall all around. The whole front of the house was covered with fruit trees, the branches of which hung over the walls, drooping with all sorts of good stuff. We stopped abruptly.

We looked first at the fruit trees, then at one another.

"I'm hungry," announced Peter for the second time, his eyes riveted on the apples and pears.

"So am I," said one of our companions, rubbing his mouth with the back of his hand.

"Me too," said one of the others, feeling his stomach tenderly.

Peter looked round cautiously. "No one's near," he said to us. "Maybe if you brought the go-car close to the wall and I stood on it—"

We all agreed to this plan except Paddy, who, as he was the eldest among us, tried to maintain some dignity in a halfhearted way. The others looked at him for leadership.

"Well?" asked Peter impatiently as Paddy said nothing. "What'll we do?"

My elder brother shuffled from one foot to the other, cleared his throat, and said with a kind of desperate solemnity, "Seventh—thou shalt not steal!"

"Sissy!" shouted the other three, making a dash for the wall. One of them bent down, legs braced, while Peter got up on to his shoulders. He reached the fruit and dropped it to the third one, who stood below holding out his coat as a blanket.

Paddy couldn't stick it any longer. He pushed my car over against the wall and climbed on to the side of it so that he had only to reach up his arm to touch the red apples and yellowish-brown pears.

"All right, that's enough—don't be greedy," said Paddy when they'd gathered a handful of apples and pears together. They climbed down, counted out the stuff among the five of us, and sat on the grassy margin of the road to eat it.

"It'll do us till we get home anyway," Peter said, feeding me a pear.

"We'll have to tell this in confession though," Paddy answered piously.

"It wasn't a real sin," said Peter, munching away at his apple. "No one will miss them—"

"Who's coming?" asked Bob, one of our two pals, his head on one side as he listened, like a dog.

We caught the sound of approaching footsteps coming along the road just round the bend.

Peter winked at us and crept to the corner, peeping round it cautiously. Then he came running back, breathless.

"Suffering duck—it's a copper!" he panted.

Paddy turned green. He seemed powerless to move. "What'll happen to us?" he asked helplessly.

"Run for it!" said Bob, leaping to his feet.

"Can't leave Christy here, can we?" Peter broke in as the steps came nearer. Then he had an idea. "Quick," he said, turning to the others. "Put all the stuff under Christy's cushion!"

There was no time for questions. In a matter of seconds they had picked up all the fruit, half dragged me out of the go-car, dumped the stuff at the bottom of it, beneath the torn old cushion, and then pushed me in on top of it.

The policeman walked round the corner and, on seeing us, came towards us slowly.

"Evening, lads," he said, smiling. He patted me on the head. "Out late, little man, eh? 'Tis almost eight."

The other four tried to keep calm, but they fidgeted uneasily and shifted their weight like hens.

"Take him home now, boys," said the friendly policeman. "Don't tarry any longer. Cheerio." With that he left us, going slowly up the road the way he had come.

They waited till he was out of sight, then they took out the apples and pears. They weren't pretty to look at.

"Aw—put 'em back!" Paddy growled when he saw them. "God didn't like us stealing them."

So, very sadly, they dumped the sticky mass of fruit

back over the wall of the big house, and we started on our way home again. We got there about ten at night, feeling as empty as air.

"Did you enjoy yourselves today?" mother asked us as we came in at the front door.

Peter looked at Paddy, Paddy looked at Peter, and they both looked at me.

"Yes," said Peter, and left it at that.

We were in better spirits the next day when Tony and Jim took me along to watch them swim in the canal not very far from our house. The day was very warm and sultry. There was hardly any sunshine, just a heavy, oppressive warmness that seemed to make the air itself a solid, palpable thing that pressed down upon you.

We got to the canal and found there was a big crowd of children gathered there, some swimming in the water, some—mostly girls—paddling in the shallow part, holding their skirts and pinafores up high above their knees, and others lying on the grassy bank, drying themselves and throwing pebbles at one another. The air was filled with the sounds of laughter and screams as they splashed about in the water, covering the roadside with spray. There was quite a crowd of spectators on the bridge.

My two brothers placed me at a point where I could see all that went on. Then they stripped themselves under the bridge, changed into togs, and took a dive into the water.

I looked on, amid all the noise and excitement, feeling hot, sticky, and a little jealous. I wanted to tear off my clothes and plunge into the water as my brothers had done.

Suddenly I felt the same way then as I had felt on that day when I first drew the letter "A"—a queer eagerness, an unconscious determination to do what the others were doing, to feel what they felt and know what they knew. I wanted more than anything else just then to go into the water.

A little while later Tony climbed out on to the bank, his body glistening and his hair clinging to his forehead.

I gave a yell, and he came up to me. In my own queer grunting language I told him I wanted to have a swim.

"G'wan—you're kidding me!" he said, laughing. I insisted. "But you'd drown!" he told me.

Nothing Tony said could make me less resolved to go into the water, being a fellow always willing to try anything once. "All right, then," he said. But when my eldest brother Jim heard, he said he'd have nothing to do with it. He wouldn't even help Tony to strip me and put togs on me.

"Give me your togs then," Tony demanded. "He can't go in in his pelt!"

He brought me behind a bush in a quiet part of the canal and there undressed me. Jim was very big and fat, and his togs were miles too large for me. Tony had to wrap them round me a few times and pin them at the back before they'd stay on. Finally, however, he got me ready and carried me down to the bank. He stopped and looked at me.

"Still want to go in?" he asked. "You won't mind if you go under and don't come up, will you?"

I grinned and shook my head. Maybe I was afraid, but I was also stubborn, too stubborn to give in now. Poor Jim stood by, trembling.

"Don't do it—you'll kill him!" he said, but we took no notice of him.

Tony pulled a branch off a tree, dipped it into the water, and waved it over my head, saying an "Our Father" over me. Then he caught me under the arms, hoisted me up a little, and swung me into the canal!

I gasped as I felt the cold, icy water rush over me. My brain became confused; everything melted into a watery blur. I was beneath the water for a second, rose, went under again, rose once more, and expected to go under for the third time. But I didn't. Instead, I lashed out frantically with my feet, and next thing I knew I was simply floating along like one of the white swans farther up the river. I kept kicking my feet out vigorously and remained sailing on top of the water. I heard a burst of laughter coming from the bank and a few moments later Tony swam up beside me. He held my arm and steered me towards the towpath, where Jim hauled me ashore. I lay there, panting but triumphant.

"You'd lick Christopher Columbus any day!" said Tony, as he knelt down and dried me.

That was my first swim. It wasn't my last, for I had many another in a little rocky stream which we discovered one summer in a wood. Often I would lie on the bank while the others were swimming or picking blackberries. Sometimes I would fall asleep there. I was happy. I looked out on the world, noticing everything except myself.

Then one day my go-car broke down: the axle snapped, the seat collapsed, and nobody could do anything with it. It was put away in the coal house to rust.

I was lost without it. My brothers could no longer bring me with them when they went out to play. Mother talked of getting me a new car when father went back to work, but I hardly heard her; I was bewildered.

It wasn't just that I missed the old car so much. It was the way I felt when I could no longer go out with my brothers. Everything was changed. I was thrown upon myself at last. That queer idea that there was something wrong which had entered my mind sometimes now loomed larger.

A few days later I was sitting in the front garden playing toy soldiers with my brothers when along came some of our pals, carrying fishing nets and jam jars on a string. They suggested we should all go fishing together. It was a good day and nobody wanted to stay at home. There was a rush for fishing rods and tackle and everybody was excited. Peter laid a bet that he would catch twenty pinkeens before the day was out.

They all crowded at the gate, ready to go. Then Tony forgot something and came back for it along with a pal. As he was going down the path again, I looked up at him dumbly, appealing silently.

He stopped. This was the first time he'd gone anywhere without me.

"Sorry, Chris," he said, not looking at me. "We'll bring you back lots of pinkeens." He moved away quickly.

"Pity about him—" began his companion. Tony gave him a violent shove that knocked him into the road. They ran on to join the others. I was left alone in the garden. I looked down at my hands twisting and twisting.

5

KATRIONA DELAHUNT

THE BOTTOM HAD fallen out of my world. Life seemed to have gone sour. Everything was different, as I saw it, and as I felt it.

Now I was seldom happy. I'd sit at the window in the kitchen and gaze out at my brothers and their pals as they played a football match on the road outside the house, seeing how Peter scored goals so often. Sometimes some of them would smile and wave at me. I'd try to wave back, but when I lifted my arm it would shoot out sideways and bang against the window frame. Then I'd throw myself onto the sofa behind me and bury my face in the corner of it.

I was now just ten, a boy who couldn't walk, speak, feed or dress himself. I was helpless, but only now did I begin to realize how helpless I really was. I still didn't know anything about myself: I knew nothing beyond the fact that I was different from others. I didn't understand what made me different or why it should be. I just knew that I couldn't run about, or play football, or climb trees, or even feed myself as the others did.

I couldn't reason this out. I couldn't even think clearly about it. I could only feel it, feel it deep down in the very core of me, like a thin sharp needle that worked its way through all the fancies and dreams of my childish mind till it tore them to shreds, leaving it naked and powerless to avoid the stark reality that I was a cripple.

Up to then I had never thought about myself. True, there had come sometimes a vague feeling that I wasn't like the others, an uneasy sort of stirring in my mind that came and went. But it was just one dark spot in the brightness of things, and I used soon to forget it. I had gone on playing with my brothers, enjoying the little bit of life which I saw, all the time unconscious of myself.

Now it was different. Now I saw everything, not through the eyes of a little boy eager for fun and brimming with curiosity, but through those of a cripple, a cripple who had only just discovered his own affliction.

I looked at Peter's hands. They were brown, steady hands with strong, square fingers, hands that could clasp a hurley firmly or swing a chestnut high into the air. Then I looked down at my own. They were queer, twisted hands with bent, crooked fingers, hands that were never still, but twitched and shook continually so that they looked more like two wriggling snakes than a pair of human hands.

I began to hate the sight of those hands, the sight of my wobbly head and lopsided mouth as I saw them in the mirror, and I soon came to hate and fear a mirror. It told me too much. It let me see what other people saw every time they looked at me—that when I opened my mouth it slid sideways, making me look ugly and foolish, that when I tried to speak I only slobbered and gabbled, the saliva running down my chin at every word I attempted to say, that my head kept shaking and wobbling from side to side, that when I'd try to smile I'd only grimace and pucker up my eyes so that my face looked like an ugly mask.

I was frightened at what I saw, because I had never thought I looked like that. I had looked in mirrors before, but, not knowing what to look for, I had seen nothing peculiar. Now every time I looked in a mirror the same grotesque face leered back at me. One day, in tears, I climbed on to my bed, reached up my left foot, and knocked the little mirror that hung on the wall off its peg and on to the floor where it smashed in bits.

Mother, hearing the crash, rushed up the stairs and asked me what had happened. I just pointed with my foot to where the shattered glass lay, the broken bits glittering like diamonds in the shaft of sunlight that came through the curtained windows.

"That means seven years of bad luck," she said, smiling, as she swept up the broken pieces of glass.

After a few weeks mother managed to buy me a new car, a proper invalid chair this time that had a nice padded seat and rubber tires. "Now you can go out again," she told me happily. I said nothing.

The next day my brothers, eager to show off my new wagon, as they called it, took me out into the streets once more. All our old pals crowded round me, each of them taking turns at pushing me along in my new car.

"Call this Mike," suggested one of them, rubbing his hand along the shining black leather arm of it.

"No," said Peter grandly with his nose in the air. "We'll call it Sylvester."

That day they took me to watch them play a football game. It was just like old times, all the gang around me, telling jokes and thinking up games to play that night. But I didn't feel the same any more. Something had gone out of me, or out of life, I couldn't tell which. I couldn't laugh with them like I used to. I kept staring into their faces to see by their looks if they noticed anything peculiar about me. I hid my face whenever anybody strange passed me by, but I couldn't help seeing how they'd glance at my face and then down at my hands, nodding their heads significantly to whoever was with them as they went on up the road, glancing back at me till they passed out of sight.

They went right through me, those looks from people in the streets. My brothers didn't think I took any notice, but I did. Even in the space of a few weeks, since my old go-car broke down, I had become as different in mind as I now knew I was in body. I had become more sensitive, more apprehensive of those I met outside my home. I looked on dumbly at my brothers and pals as they played around me, not even using my grunt now. I found no pleasure in their games: I had become a spectator now instead of one of the participants.

After that day I went out no more, except, perhaps, once or twice a year, and even then I'd only let them take me out to quiet lonely places where there were no houses or people. My brothers didn't understand what made me such a stay-at-home. They appealed to me again and again to go out with them and have fun like before, but I just shook my head and smiled at them. Then they'd scratch their heads, shrug their shoulders, and go out themselves.

Mother noticed the change in me and I believe she knew the cause of it, but she didn't say anything. She understood me better than anyone else at home. I couldn't deceive her, because she always had an uncanny way of finding out whether I was happy or sad, as though she could feel half of what I felt. She saw now that I was nearly always sad, moody, and shut up in myself. I didn't crawl about the house as I used to, but sat curled up in the big armchair, staring at the fire or merely at the wall.

She tried hard to make up for it, for she saw I was lonely and knew the danger of letting loneliness stay with me. So she devised little pastimes for me, like writing out stories from the newspapers into cheap six-penny copy-books with a lead pencil held in my left foot. She'd go over them to see if I had copied them down correctly. The writing would be awful: huge, scrawling capitals sloping horizontally down the page with no dots, dashes or commas between them and, of course, no such thing as a question or exclamation mark anywhere.

Still, though it helped to lighten the days for me, it could not take away that awful dissatisfied feeling that was beginning to take root in my heart. Writing, or rather copying, was all right; it helped to make me interested in reading at least. But it wasn't enough. I wanted something else, something that would give me a chance to expend some of the nervous energy, some of the tautness and mental tension that welled up inside me. I soon got tired of merely copying what other people had written and I looked around for some other way in which to express myself. I felt terribly bottled up.

I was now ten and a half and beginning to sink deeper and deeper into myself. Mother tried, but nothing could rouse me, nothing could bring back the happy child that used to be me. He didn't exist any more. In his place was a tense, silent, great-eyed creature who had nerves as sharp as broken glass and as taut as telegraph wires.

Then, one Christmas, one of us—I think it was Paddy —got a box of paints from Santa Claus. That same year I got a box of toy soldiers, but the moment I saw Paddy's paints with all the wonderful colors, and the long, slender, fuzzy-haired brush, I fell in love with them at once. I felt I must have them to keep as my own. I was fascinated by the little solid blocks of paint—blue, red, yellow, green, and white. Later in the day I sat and watched Paddy as he tried to make some impression with the paints on a piece of white cardboard torn from an old shoe box, but he only made a mess, and in a queer way I felt annoyed with him —and a bit jealous.

"Blow—I can't use these things!" he grumbled, flinging his brush down. "They're only for girls."

I saw my chance. Pushing out my box of lead soldiers towards him with my foot, I asked him, in grunts, to swap them for his paints.

"Done!" exclaimed Paddy, glad to get rid of such a sissy's toy. "But how are you going to use them?"

I didn't know that myself, but I just lifted my left foot and smiled.

I put them away till all the excitement of Christmas was past. Then one quiet afternoon, when there was nobody in the kitchen but mother and myself, I crawled over to the press, opened the door with my foot, and took the little black box of paints out and laid it on the floor in front of me.

"What are you up to?" said mother, coming over to where I squatted with my back against the wall. "Surely you're not trying to paint!"

I nodded very solemnly. I picked up the brush between my toes, wetted it in my mouth, then rubbed it on one of the paint squares—the bright blue one which I liked best. I next rubbed the brush against my other foot—and saw a blue spot on it when I took it away.

"It works!" I managed to exclaim, and I could feel my face hot with excitement.

"I'll get you water," said mother, going into the pantry

and coming back with a cupful which she put on the floor beside me.

I had no paper. Mother got me some by tearing a page out of Peter's sum-copy. I dipped the brush into the water and rubbed on some vivid red paint. Then I steadied my foot and, while mother looked on intently, painted on the open page before me—the outline of a cross.

I grinned triumphantly up at her. I remembered how, on that day five years previously, we had sat together on the floor, almost in the same spot, while I shook and sweated as I drew with my left foot for the first time. Mother had been there at my side then—she was at my side now, still inspiring me.

There was no sweating or shaking this time. I did it quite smoothly. I was holding a paintbrush now, not a broken piece of chalk. But it meant the same thing—I had discovered a new way to communicate with the outside world, a new way to talk with my left foot.

As time went on, I became more and more devoted to my little box of paints. I painted all sorts of crazy things, from a sketch of Peter's face—to which he indignantly objected—to a bunch of dead fish lying in the dustbin, done before Tibby, the cat from next door, finished them off.

Then mother managed to buy me some more paints and brushes, along with one or two drawing books and a pencil. This, of course, broadened my range of expression and allowed me to have a greater choice of subject. After the first few weeks of uncertainty and awkwardness, I settled down contentedly with my new pastime. I painted every day upstairs in the back bedroom, completely by myself.

I was changing. I didn't know it then, but I had found a way to be happy again and to forget some of the things that had made me unhappy. Above all I learned to forget myself. I didn't miss going out with my brothers now, for I had something to keep my mind active, something to make each day a thing to look forward to.

I would sit crouched on the floor for hours, holding the brush between my toes, my right leg curled up under my left, my arms held tightly at my sides, the hands clenched. All my paints and brushes were around me, and I would get mother or father to pin the drawing paper to the floor with tacks to keep it steady. It looked a very queer awkward position, with my head almost between my knees and my back as crooked as a corkscrew. But I painted all my best pictures in this way, with the wooden floor as my only easel.

Slowly I began to lose my early depression: I had a feeling of pure joy while I painted, a feeling I had never experienced before and which seemed almost to lift me above myself. It was only when I wasn't painting that I became depressed and cross with everyone at home. At first mother thought she was doing the right thing in encouraging me to paint, thinking it would give me less time to become unhappy. But after a while she began to worry, because I was spending so much time alone. I'd sit for hours painting in the bedroom upstairs, unconscious of everything—including myself.

She often came up the stairs to see if I wanted anything, coming on tiptoe into the room. There she'd find me, bent over a picture, the brush in my toes. Sometimes she'd come over to brush the hair out of my eyes and wipe the sweat from my forehead, for although I could now use my left foot as easily as Peter or Paddy could use their hands, it was still a terrific strain on the rest of my body to sit on the floor crouched over a picture for almost the whole day. But often when mother came up to see if I was all right, I'd just nod my head curtly and grunt.

Then one day, when I was about eleven, mother became ill and was shifted to the Rotunda Hospital where, a few weeks later, she gave birth to her last child, a boy, thus completing the total of twenty-two. She remained very ill after my smallest brother was born and rapidly became worse. We were all in a terrible state at home. With mother away the house seemed to go dead. It was like taking away the inside of a clock, leaving the hands still and powerless. I didn't even paint now. I had no interest in anything because I thought mother was going to die.

I was huddled up on the sofa one cold night in December when a knock sounded on the front door. Father, who was sitting by the fire holding a newspaper closely in his hand, too worried to read it, didn't hear the knock the first time, but when it sounded again he got up and went into the hall to answer it.

I heard voices at the hall door, but I didn't bother to listen, being too worried and upset because of mother. I had just turned over on my side, burying my head in the corner of the sofa nearest the wall, when the door was opened and I heard father and someone else come into the kitchen.

"This is Christy," father said. Then I heard a girl's voice saying: "Is he asleep?"

In a dazed way I looked up at the visitor, blinking a little. The light hadn't been switched on yet and the room was a bit shadowy, but by the light of the street lamp outside I saw that my visitor was a young girl, perhaps about eighteen. She was slim and tall and lovely—the most beautiful girl I had ever seen.

"Hello," she said, smiling a lovely smile. "My name is Miss Delahunt. Your mother told me about you."

I tried to say something, but I only made the same queer grunting noise that I always made when I tried to speak. The girl just smiled and sat down on the edge of the sofa.

"I thought I'd call and meet you," she said. "You don't mind, do you?"

I shook my head vigorously. Then she told me how she had heard of me. I learned she was an almoner's student at the Rotunda Hospital, that she had met mother and heard about me and how I painted with my left foot, and so had wanted to meet me. Also she had another motive in coming. Mother was very worried about how we were getting on at home without her, so the girl had decided to come out and get me to write mother a little note.

"Will you do that for me?" she asked.

I couldn't refuse. Then father lifted me on to the table and, holding the pencil between my toes, I wrote on the back of an old envelope:

"Dear Mom. Don't worry. All okay. Lots of grub. Get well soon. Christy."

I didn't want to put any kisses at the end of it, but she

told me it would look better if I did, so, unwillingly, I scrawled one big kiss in the corner of the envelope and gave it to her.

She left, but promised to come again. I went to bed that night feeling dizzy.

Next time she came I got a big surprise, for she brought me out a whole load of paints, brushes and drawing books, along with the good news that mother was improving and would be home soon.

Katriona Delahunt—came into my life at a time when I most needed someone like her, someone quite apart from my own path of life who would make me realize the necessity of trying to rise above the ordinary standard of thought and activity around me and so help me attain a securer balance within myself. Apart from mother, she was to be my greatest inspiration in the years and the struggles that lay before me.

But of course I didn't know all this at eleven years old. I only knew that I had met my first dream-girl.

6

THE ARTIST

MEETING MY FIRST dream-girl was an event which for me had a unique chain of consequences. I was too young to know if my heart misbehaved itself in any way, and too young to notice it if it did, for at that age I centered my interest more in my left foot than in any other part of me—my heart included.

And yet, I suppose my feelings were much the same as those of any other young chap with the least bit of imagination in him. Although at first I got confused and self-conscious when Miss Delahunt came to visit me, I gradually became calmer and, indeed, began to look forward very excitedly to the days when she would come. I'd get mother to comb my hair very carefully, instructing her to put as many waves in it as she could. Sometimes I, too, like Peter, would get mother to pinch some of Tony's eight-penny bottle of hair oil to put in my hair whenever I knew she was coming.

I still couldn't talk, but somehow or other speech didn't seem to matter an awful lot when I was with my new friend. We seemed to have a strange unconscious language of our own, a peculiar way of understanding each other without consciously expressing ourselves. I knew nothing about telepathy at that time, but even so I do not think it would accurately describe the way I could converse with Miss Delahunt without even having to grunt.

My mind began to stretch itself. I understood more about myself and the scenes that went on about me, not because anyone told me about them, but because I had begun to feel a little more, think a little more, and therefore to know a little more. I had come to know myself better because I had learned to express myself and to reach down into all that lay below the surface of my mind. But I was still quite ignorant of myself in the light of all that was to come.

As I became further attached to painting I began to feel happier and more tranquil within myself. I was less inclined to snap at the others if they asked me anything or even spoke to me, as I did before. Painting became the one great love in my life, the main pivot of my concentration. I lived within the orbit of my paints and brushes.

Yet it wasn't just painting that made me so happy. That in itself would not have been sufficient. It was the fact that I painted, not just to please myself, but to please someone else: the feeling of being useful, of painting my pictures for somebody who had become a sort of goddess in my eyes. My lovely dream-girl not only was always very pleased to accept my little paintings, but she actually *looked forward* to them. That was the great thing about her: she had a knack of making me feel important, of making me feel useful and responsible. I painted very badly. All I did or could do were horrible little landscapes with great lumps of brown and green scattered all over the paper and a huge sticky sea of blue for the sky. But Miss Delahunt always spoke of them as if they had been great masterpieces, and with this encouragement I began painting better and with greater confidence.

I mixed all my own colors. I arranged my paints on the floor and prepared my pencils and brushes—all with my left foot. The folk at home were willing enough to help me in doing this, but I couldn't trust them because none of them knew the first thing about paints or brushes or how to handle them. I was afraid they might do something terrible to my precious equipment, so I preferred to look after it myself.

At first I used to store all my paints in an old cardboard box and keep it under my bed. But father made me a wooden box to keep them in and I called this my "toolbox."

Then one December day a few weeks before Christmas, I was flicking over the pages of the *Sunday Independent* with my foot when I saw the announcement of a Christmas painting competition for children from twelve to sixteen. I was just a little past twelve so I was quite eligible to enter. It was a Sunday morning, all the others were out at mass, and mother was in the pantry washing cabbage for the dinner, while father sat at the window reading his paper. I looked at the announcement again. There was an ordinary black-and-white reproduction of the picture that had to be colored, showing a gay ballroom scene and Cinderella dancing with her Prince Charming in the middle of the floor, surrounded by the other dancers, all in elegant costumes, the men in skintight stockings and doublets and the ladies in flowing skirts. Over their heads swung great chandeliers.

I thought it would be a good picture to paint, and I was so attracted by it that I seemed to see it all finished and glowing with color as I stared at it. I saw it all so plainly that I felt I had already done it.

I called mother in from the pantry and showed her the news about the competition.

"Try it," she said. I shook my head and mumbled something about not being good enough. "That's silly," said mother. "You don't have to be a genius. Just try."

I did. I painted the picture that same afternoon and I did it better than I thought I would. I paid Cinderella special attention. I made her quite a glamour girl, with pink cheeks, golden ringlets and a beautiful blue dress. Her white satin slippers peeped daintily from under her gown, like two little mice. I painted Prince Charming's uniform a bright purple and, as an artistic touch, I decided to bespatter it with tiny spots of yellow in imitation of gems. I painted both their eyes blue, though I put a spot of green in the Prince's.

I was satisfied when I had finished the picture. I didn't want to have anything to do with the competition itself because I didn't think I stood a chance. But, although I could refuse to listen to mother, I couldn't refuse to do whatever my dream-girl asked, and when mother told her about the competition and showed her the picture I had colored, Miss Delahunt said I should enter it without delay. To me it was an ultimatum.

I went over the picture more carefully, adding a few touches here and there and, on the whole, toning it up a little more. Then I got mother to seal, stamp, and post it away to the newspaper offices the next day.

I really thought it was all a waste of time and I soon forgot about it. I hadn't a hope in the world of winning even one of the small consolation prizes. I just went back to painting in the ordinary way all that week, happy that at least I had pleased Miss Delahunt by doing what she had asked me, though I thought it was useless.

Then, on the following Friday morning, there came a knock on the front door. Mother was in the pantry, washing some clothes, and she came in to answer it with her hands covered with soapsuds. I happened at the time to be perched on the big round table in the kitchen, painting, with all my paints and brushes around me. This was an unusual place for me to paint, for I preferred to do my work upstairs in the bedroom where I could be alone. But that particular morning I had decided to paint in the kitchen just as a change.

Mother answered the knock and found it was a newspaper reporter along with a photographer from the *Independent* who had come to see me. It transpired that without my knowing of it Miss Delahunt had gone to the newspaper people and told them that one of the pictures sent in to their office was done by a boy who painted with his toes. They had been a little skeptical of this and decided to send out one of their reporters to check on it and see what it was all about.

When the reporter and photographer came into the kitchen, I was just putting the finishing touches to a tropical South Sea island in a blue lagoon, complete with waving palms and golden-brown beaches. Hearing the door being opened, I looked up: the two press men stood and stared across the room at me, with mother a little behind them. I became confused and went on painting quickly.

"It's true!" I heard one of them exclaim in a sort of awed whisper.

The two of them were then brought over by mother and I found out who they were.

"We found it hard to believe, Mrs. Brown," they said, "but now . . ."

They asked mother many questions about me, and as she told them my little story up to that age, they became more incredulous than before. All the time this was going on, I painted on quietly, trying to be as calm as I could. At length they took a photograph of me sitting on the table with a paintbrush between my toes and an easel before me. I had been made a present of that easel by a friend some months before. It was very useful, but I much preferred to paint on the floor and the easel was put in only on account of the occasion, to make me look more like an artist. It was my first photograph.

The next Sunday morning I was lying cozily in bed with Peter, halfway between sleep and wakefulness, when father ran up the stairs, burst into the room, and pulled me up into a sitting position.

"Look—look!" he said, waving a copy of the *Sunday Independent* before my face. "See—you've won!"

It was true. There, on the center page, was the photo-

graph they had taken of me the previous Friday. In it was
a little boy in short trousers, his thin legs bent under one
another, his eyebrows cocked up rather snobbishly, and
by his side one twisted hand held tightly to keep it still.

I was brought down to the kitchen where all the family
were eating breakfast and talking excitedly about my success. As father carried me into the room, everyone stopped
speaking at once. Mother laid down the teapot she was
holding and came up to me as father held me in his arms.

"Never stop trying, Chris," she said as she kissed me.

And my dream-girl?—she came too, later on in the day.
She took my hand in hers and kissed me on the forehead,
saying she was proud of me.

7

A LOOK OF PITY

THIRTEEN—AND STILL very much the boy artist who
hadn't yet discovered himself or come to know his own
abilities sufficiently to make use of them. Painting became
everything to me. By it I learned to express myself in
many subtle ways. Through it I made articulate all that
I saw and felt, all that went on inside the mind that was
housed within my useless body like a prisoner in a cell
looking out on a world that hadn't yet become a reality
to me.

I saw more with my mind than with my eyes. I'd sit for
hours sometimes, alone in my bedroom, not painting or
doing anything else, but just sitting and staring into a
world of my own, away and beyond everything that made
up my ordinary life. When I went into one of those day-
dreams I forgot everything else: the loud voices in the
stuffy little kitchen below . . . Peter trying to play the
mouth organ on the doorstep . . . the sound of jazz music

coming from the wireless downstairs . . . the high shrill voice of the ragman in the street outside. . . . They all melted and faded into one confused blurring noise, and then, gradually, I'd hear nothing more or see nothing more. I'd just sit there, thinking. . . .

I didn't go out at all now. I had stopped going out a long time ago. I didn't even play in the house with my brothers any more. This puzzled them at first, but they slowly began to accept the new kind of relationship that had developed between us. I didn't become a stranger to the rest of the family, of course, because with so many of us all living together in the same house that was impossible; we all formed part of one another, so to speak. But I had come to live more within myself. I lived *with* the others, but at the same time I lived *apart* from them, apart from all the things that meant most to them. I was happy by myself, but I didn't know then how far I really was from being self-sufficient.

And yet, withdrawn as I was from the ordinary life of a boy, the life of the streets and back alleys, I found that my heart was still miles ahead of my body in growth and development: I lost it again, good and truly this time. Another dream-girl had come into my vision, not as tall and beautiful as my old one, but more my own age. She was called Jenny. She lived a few doors away from my house. She was small, energetic, gay, with a mass of brown curls framing her pretty elfin face with its lively green eyes and pouting lips. Unfortunately, Jenny was a coquette. She could start a riot among all the boys on our street by just using those lovely eyes of hers in the right way. They were all crazy about her and there were many fights when they started arguing about who would marry her when they grew up into men.

I didn't go out any more, but that didn't stop me from seeing Jenny. I worshipped her from afar, that is, from my bedroom window. It made me lazy in my painting, for whenever I heard Jenny's voice in the street below I'd crawl over to the window and sit on the bed, gazing out at her as she ran and skipped about with the other girls, whom I didn't notice at all. One day she looked up at me as I sat gazing down on her. I felt my face grow hot and made to draw back, but at that moment she smiled. I managed to smile back, and then she threw me a kiss. I could hardly believe my eyes when she did this, but she did it again before running away down the street, her dark curls flying and her white dress blowing in the wind.

That night I tore a page from an old jotter and, holding the pencil in my shaking toes, I wrote a passionate little note to Jenny which I got one of my younger brothers to deliver, threatening him with my foot if he didn't give it to Jenny herself. I told her in the note that I thought she was the prettiest kid on our street and that I'd paint her lots of pictures if she'd let me. Then, in a hurried post-script, I told her that I loved her "lots and lots of times."

I waited for my brother to come back in excitement and fear, not daring to hope that Jenny would reply. In a half an hour's time he returned—with a note from her tucked up his jersey!

I took the note and read it eagerly, quite forgetful of my brother, who stood by, staring at me in a funny way as if he thought I'd gone mad or something. I read Jenny's little letter over and over again, especially the part where she said she'd come and see me in my back yard the next day if I wanted her to. There was a queer fluttering inside me and a lightness in my head. I felt myself go hot and cold in turn. After a while I looked up. My brother was still standing with his hands behind his back and his mouth open, a look of bewilderment in his big blue eyes as he fixed them on my face. I yelled at him to scram, and he scuttled from the room like a startled rabbit. Then I threw myself back on the pillow and sighed, my heart jumping crazily.

I kept the appointment next day, all spruce and "done up" with Tony's de luxe hair grease actually dripping down my forehead. Little Jenny was very sweet. We sat and looked over some of my paintings, and she gave a little gasp of admiration at each one I showed her. I was shy and awkward at first because of my slurred speech and the way I used my foot instead of my hands. But Jenny was either a very innocent person or a very tactful one, for she didn't seem to notice anything queer about me, but talked on gaily to me about games and parties and the boy next door the same as if I had been Peter or Paddy. I liked her for that.

We became great pals, Jenny and I. We never said a great deal to each other, but we exchanged innumerable little notes each week and she'd steal over to see me every Saturday night, bringing me little books and magazines which I never read but which I treasured very much, storing them all away in the old worm-eaten cupboard in my bedroom.

I was secretly proud that I, a cripple, had made friends with the prettiest and most sought-after girl in our neighborhood. I often heard Peter saying fervently that Jenny was a peach and that he'd do anything to be her favorite beau. Every time I heard this I felt very proud of myself and enormously vain, thinking myself quite a conqueror, because it was not I who went to Jenny, but Jenny who came to me!

Peter became suspicious, and one Saturday he came upon Jenny and me as we sat together in the back yard, our heads very close to one another, although we were only looking at some old storybook that Jenny had brought along. I got red in the face, but Jenny didn't move: she just lifted her head, smiled at my brother briefly, and bent over the book again. Peter gave me a murderous look and went into the house, banging the door after him.

That evening, before she left, Jenny sat very quietly, toying idly with the book, a little frown creasing her forehead and her lower lip pushed out, as she always looked when she wanted to say something difficult. After a little while she got up, hesitated, then suddenly knelt down on the grass beside me and kissed me very tenderly on the forehead. I drew back, surprised, bewildered, for she had never kissed me before.

I opened my mouth to try and say something, but at that moment Jenny sprang to her feet, her face flushed and her eyes wet with tears, and rushed from the garden, her small black shoes clattering noisily as she ran down the stone path and disappeared into the street.

She didn't come for weeks after this, and I didn't hear from her although I fairly bombarded her with notes. In the meantime Peter tried to discourage me by telling me many wicked tales about poor little Jenny, but I didn't believe him a bit, not even when he told me that she made every one of the boys pay her a penny for every kiss she gave them.

"That's why I'm always broke!" he said mournfully, his hands stuck in his empty pockets.

I often sat up in my bed at night, thinking of Jenny and the way she kissed me that day in the back garden. I felt very melancholy and alone. Why doesn't she come, I asked myself, as I tossed restlessly in the dark, hearing Peter snoring comfortably at my side.

My fourteenth birthday came along, and among the other birthday cards I got that morning there was one written in a small childish hand which was Jenny's, but still she never came to see me. I often saw her from my bedroom window playing in the streets below, but she kept her eyes away from my house and never looked up once. I'd sit at the window for hours, hoping she'd glance up at me, until the twilight came and everything grew dark and I could see nothing more save the dim whiteness of her frock as she ran along the street with the other girls while a laughing crowd of boys chased after them.

To hide my disappointment I painted furiously for the whole of every day, painting crazy little pictures that had neither pattern nor theme. They were just haphazard slices of my boiling mind dashed on to the paper wildly and recklessly.

Then one day, as I sat disconsolately in the back yard with my back against a soapbox, I heard a step close by. I looked up wearily. It was Jenny. She stood a few feet away, at the entrance to the yard, her slim, childish figure outlined against the white wall behind her, vividly bright in the June sunshine, her shadow falling crookedly on the warm concrete ground. She was looking across at me, but —it was a look of pity.

I knew then, as I came to know many times later, how bitter and crushing a simple look of pity can be to some-

one like myself who needs something other than sympathy
—the strength that only genuine human affection can give
to the weakest heart.

I lowered my head under her pitying gaze and, without
a word being said on either side, Jenny turned slowly and
left me to myself in the yard.

I became different after that. For a few blissful weeks I
had allowed myself to dream that I was a normal, ordinary
boy of fourteen who thought himself in love with the
sweetest girl in the whole neighborhood and who was
foolish enough and vain enough to think that she cared
for him in return. Now all that make-believe was at an
end, but the bitterest of all was the realization that I had
tricked myself into believing that my affliction didn't matter, that my "queerness" was merely self-consciousness
which nobody else took any notice of. I saw what an ass I
had been to fool myself so magnificently.

In the excitement of meeting Miss Delahunt, the novelty
of painting, and the dreamy enchantment that came with
Jenny, I had almost forgotten myself. I had come to believe that there was no difference between myself and
other people, except in my own mind. It was great
pleasure to lose myself in such a dream world, in such an
impossible paradise. It was pure joy to blind my eyes to
every unpleasant fact about myself, even for a few brief
weeks. But—it made the coming back to reality all the
more violent and bitter.

Life at home was changing, too. It seemed to me that
everyone had grown up all of a sudden. It was a shock to
realize that Jim and Tony were now men. Jim, the quiet
boy that everyone made fun of, with his easygoing ways
and girlish tenderness. And Tony, the daredevil, who had
always enjoyed a certain superiority over the rest of us at
home because he was never afraid to speak with his fists
at the least opportunity. Lily was no longer the little dark-
haired sister who had often wheeled me on a Sunday
morning along the banks of the canal, putting pennies on
my eyes to make me go to sleep. She had suddenly become a woman, engaged to be married. Paddy was no
longer a schoolboy in short trousers and catapult sticking

out of his back pocket, but an apprentice bricklayer who marched in proudly every Friday night with his pay packet and handed it with great pomposity to mother, his boots and overalls begrimed with dust and mortar. Mona had changed from a plump, fluffy-haired little girl with fat cheeks and pudgy hands into a pretty young lady of seventeen with lipstick and powder and enormous high heels who had a different date almost every night and who loved to go dancing better than anything else.

Peter was a year younger than I, and I had always looked upon him as my favorite brother, because being almost the same age we could hit and shout at each other without any restraint, and thus he came to know me better than any of the others. But to my eyes even he had changed, even he had grown into long trousers, thus becoming a different person, a little more dignified and therefore a lot more inaccessible.

I seemed to have no link, no affinity at all with my younger brothers and sisters. They had their own childhood to live through and their own pals to make, just as I had once. They were good kids, but they seemed to be a little in awe of their crippled brother and perhaps, rather unconsciously, afraid of him at the same time. They knew me very little, because I painted all day in my bedroom and saw little of them except on Sundays when I'd sit on the sofa in the kitchen looking through the Sunday papers before listening to mass on the radio, and even then I didn't say much to them, partly because I couldn't talk very well, but mostly because I never had anything to say.

Before I knew it, my fifteenth birthday had come around. Mother managed to give a party. It was a gay turnout and some of my old pals came along. Unknown to me, my sister Mona had invited Jenny to it, and she came. She was not the small, freckled-faced Jenny that I had known in our back-yard romance, but a lovely sweet sixteen, a smiling young girl in a gray satin frock, her nails polished and her dark hair scented. I looked at her across the table and our eyes met. But whatever little resemblance she had to the old Jenny vanished the next moment when she came over to me and took my hand without the least sign of hesitation or shyness.

"How are you, Christy—well?" she asked me in a half-frolicsome, half-placating way. "Yes, yes, that's good, don't excite yourself," she said soothingly as I strove to say something. I almost hated her for that.

After the little party was over and they had all gone, mother asked me if I had enjoyed it. I told her I had. It was a lie, for my head was aching painfully. But worse than the headache, worse than anything else, was the terrible heartache I felt as I lay down to sleep that night.

I knew I was a child no longer, but neither was I grownup. I was poised between the blissful ignorance of childhood and the awakening pain and frustration of adolescence. I longed to be ignorant and happy as before. But I knew childhood had gone. I had seen the hopelessness and futility of my future that day in the back yard when a child gazed on me with a look of pity in her eyes.

8

THE PRISON WALLS

I COULD NOW no longer run away from myself. I had grown too big for that. In a thousand ways, large and small, as each day went by, as the family grew up one by one and became—to me—strange, self-supporting adults, I saw and felt the limitations, the boredom, the terrible *narrowness* of my own existence. All around me were signs of activity, effort, growth. Everyone had something to do, something to occupy them and keep their minds and their hands active. They had interests, activities, and aims to make their lives an integrated whole and give their energies a natural outlet and a natural medium of expression. I had only my left foot.

My life seemed just like a dark, stuffy little corner in which I was thrust with my face turned towards the wall, hearing all the sound and motion of the big world outside, and yet unable to move, unable to go out and take my place in it like my brothers and sisters and everyone else that I knew. I felt as if I was merely moving along a groove, thinking the same things, feeling the same things, dreading the same things. I was shut in, cut off, bottled up. I was left with nothing but frustrated tryings and little narrow thoughts.

Mother was always a tremendous well of inspiration to me, but now we didn't always agree with each other. We had many quarrels. The only thing I could say plainly and without any difficulty was "go to hell," and I sometimes said it to mother when we were having one of our rows and I was in a temper.

Speech was a strange, awkward thing with me, but I didn't need any words for mother to know what was going on inside me. I believe she could almost read my thoughts. There was a queer, almost uncanny, sort of link between us that could make the one wince at what the other felt, as the two decapacitated limbs of a spider will move and jerk as long as life remains in either of them, though they be yards apart.

She knew I had growing pains, that I was feeling my own position in life more acutely as I got older, and she sought to soften the reality of it a little, to give me her own strength and spirit, if only by showing me that I wasn't alone, that she *knew*. She was something more than a mother to me; she was a comrade in arms.

Katriona Delahunt was also a great help. To my adolescent mind she spoke of something so beautiful and elevated that I wondered sometimes if she was real, if she wasn't some lovely illusion or apparition that would suddenly vanish away.

But I knew she was real when I heard her voice in my ears, when I saw the tints of light in her brown hair, and saw her smiling when she looked at me as I sat painting one of my pictures to give to her. No, she wasn't one of my dreams, but a beautiful reality.

I went on painting my little water colors, painting things I had never seen, but only imagined, like landscapes, village scenes, ships, trees beside a pond in a park, and so on. But now even painting had changed, like everything else. It couldn't satisfy me any more. I still *liked* it, but I had ceased to *love* it. There was something in me, some new energy, some new need, that couldn't be expressed by just putting bright reds and yellows and somber browns on to paper and working them into a pattern: I needed something else, some broader medium to speak through. My mind had become bigger and my scope in painting had dwindled to a mere pinpoint. Every day I became more desperate. I couldn't speak with my lips, and now I found I couldn't speak through painting either. I felt as if I were being slowly suffocated.

I remembered how sad I had been as a child when I first found out that I was different from other people. I thought the world had ended for me then. But only now was I beginning to feel the full significance of that difference, the true meaning of it. As a child I had cried bitterly when I became conscious of my own crippledom. I didn't cry now—I hadn't the comfort of tears. All my agony was inside.

One day, in a fit of despair, frightened and bewildered by all I felt, I crawled up the stairs and into my bedroom, and bolted the door. Then I got pencil and paper out of my box, sat down on the bed and began to write. I had decided to do away with myself that day by throwing myself from the bedroom window into the concrete yard below. But before doing this, I was going to write a confession, a sort of "last will and testament" to leave behind me. I picked up the pencil grandly and began magnificently.

"To Whom it may Concern—knowing nobody is concerned. . . ."

That was a grand opening phrase, I thought. I finished the note, folded it neatly, and left it on the pillow. Then I crawled nearer the window, opened it with my left foot and looked out. I hadn't thought the house was so high before, the ground seemed a thousand feet below the level of the window, though it was actually only about twelve feet. It was a cold day and there was a strong wind blowing. I felt it rush against my face as I looked out, so that I could hardly breathe. I put out one leg. Then I thought of the way Peter and I used to play as children with our toy soldiers in the back garden in the summer evenings, stalking each other warily through the tall grass. . . . Now I braced myself manfully and put out my other leg. Now, for no reason, I recalled the Christmas when poor father had played Santa Claus when he could hardly walk straight, and how he had fallen over Paddy's boots in the dark and started to sing "Kathleen Mavourneen" as he lay on the floor with all the toys around him. . . . I took a deep breath and pulled myself upwards so that now I was actually sitting on the window with my feet dangling in space. I shut my eyes. . . . It would be an awful big drop, but I was going to do it. Nothing could stop me now. Then I thought of Katriona Delahunt. . . . I got down from the window and began to cry like a baby.

I was now sixteen. Lily had married, so, too, had Tony after a whirlwind romance. Jim was the next to join the married ranks, and I suspected Paddy was courting from the way he tried to lecture Peter on how to go about the difficult business of getting girl friends, though Peter, sticking out his chest, would tell Paddy that he could give him a few practical hints on the subject himself. Mona went dancing every night and was nearly always in the wars with father because she didn't agree with him that eleven o'clock at night was late enough for her to be out. Many times she'd come home late, opening the hall door noiselessly, slipping off her high-heeled shoes and going up the stairs as softly as a cat in her nyloned feet, only to be met on the landing by father.

A year later Peter left school and went to work as another bricklayer, apprenticed to Jim. Father was quite determined that all his sons should become bricklayers like himself, not stopping even to argue if they had thought of taking up any other occupation. So far he had succeeded, as Jim, Tony, Paddy, and Peter were now all bricklayers, earning good money.

"He'd make the best bricklayer of the lot of you," father would say when he was a little tight, pointing at me in front of the others. "You'd be earning five pounds a week now, Chris, building houses, a pair of dungarees on you and a good steel trowel in your hand." I hated bricklaying because I couldn't lay bricks.

After some months, a new feeling sprang up within me —a horrible feeling. I began to be not merely miserable and gloomy, but also resentful. I resented the world as a whole because of my twisted mouth and hands, and useless limbs. I looked about at all that was normal and perfect around me, and asked myself for the hundredth time why was I made different, why should I have been given the same feelings, the same needs and sensitivities as other people along with a practically functionless body that not only denied me the right to live a normal life, but also made me sick at the very sight of myself. What had I to look forward to? What prospect had I of being anything other than the cripple who painted with his toes? People always thought it was a marvelous thing that I could paint with my toes and told me I was lucky, yes, quite a remarkable boy. But what difference did painting with my left foot make? What good was it saying I was remarkable? I didn't want to be remarkable—I only wanted to be ordinary, like everyone else. Just because I did with my left foot what others did with their hands, people said it was a wonderful thing. Maybe it was—I didn't know. I used my foot simply because I couldn't use my hands, but it did not make me feel proud or unique. In fact I never used my left foot in the presence of anybody I didn't know very well, because it made me feel rather silly and awkward. I always felt like a performing monkey or seal.

Then suddenly one day I had an idea. I had always been fond of writing letters, mostly of course to Katriona Delahunt. I still remember writing her little epistles that were mostly concerned with horses and descriptions of mother's new baby. But now I decided to try something more ambitious, not just letters, but stories. The idea grew and grew till it invaded my whole mind.

I hadn't read much before this. Books were rare phe-

nomena in our house. Bread was thought more important.
Feeding our bellies seemed a more vital job to us than
trying to feed our minds. Still, I had lots of ideas crowding
my mind which I couldn't express through my paints and
brushes. The sudden inspiration to try and pin them
down on paper through the use of words came to me as I
lay on my bed one wintry day, holding a bit of straw between my toes and making idle designs with it on the rain-
washed window.

Immediately, I got a sixpenny jotter and began to write.
I hardly knew what I was doing. I just sat there, writing
down whatever came into my head. It was a crazy jumble
of words, sentences, and paragraphs that hadn't the least
relation to one another. It was just like mixing my paints
and letting them all run into one mass of color. I played
with words like a child fascinated by a new toy, writing
them down on the paper and then looking at them in a
sort of wonder.

Later I began to connect them, and then tried to weave
them into a pattern, just like I did with my paints. Finally
I started to put thoughts behind what I wrote, so that in a
little while they were not merely words but ideas, not
merely disconnected figures, but thoughts.

I had first learned to write with my toes when I was five
years old, but I had to wait till I was almost seventeen
before I realized that it could give me the key to a new
sort of life, that with it I could explore new realms of
thought and build for myself a world in which I might
live alone, independent of others. Just as Peter and the
rest built their houses with bricks, so could I now build,
not just a house, but a whole world of my own, not a
world of bricks and mortar but a grand new world of
thought and ideas.

From then on writing became my only real interest.
Just as the paintbrush used to be my scepter, so now a
pencil was seldom out of my foot. I wrote stories about
the American Wild West, made up of tremendous physical
action and rolling wagons. These were mostly based on
memories of my childhood days at the "pictures." The
characters in them were tobacco-chewing, gun-slinging

men who rode all day and drank all night, and girls with streamlined figures and roving eyes who never seemed to do anything except kick up their legs and drink gin.

Often I'd start a story with about twenty characters in it, but about halfway through I'd become confused and wouldn't know what to do with them all, so I'd let them all be shot in turn till only about two of the main ones were left. My jotter would often become a graveyard.

Then I started to be sentimental and wrote wistful little tales based on a boy-meets-girl theme. These were dreamy and full of wishful thinking, and although I enjoyed the actual writing of them they always left me sad and on edge afterwards when I remembered that, though I might imagine such things vividly enough to write about them, I would never experience them myself in real life.

I even attempted to write detective thrillers in which bullets and dead bodies abounded. Any time I felt really depressed, I'd pick my pencil up and write morbid descriptions of decomposing corpses being found in cellars and attics, or of screams ringing out suddenly in the dead of night in damp old country mansions.

I was always melodramatic, and in those early attempts, not being content merely to murder my characters, I murdered them in the stickiest way possible. Shooting them wasn't enough, I sliced them up into little pieces and scattered their remains about. It was very gory.

I don't think I was happy, even now, but at least I was occupied, I had found a way to deaden the monotony of every day. It was just like opening a bottle of ginger pop and letting all the pent-up bubbles escape. I felt life had become a little less stuffy.

But always, whatever I did, wherever I turned, I felt lonely and restless. It was like living in chains. As my mind developed, it grew more conscious of my body, till the knowledge of its disabilities was enough to give me an almost physical sense of pain. There was no such thing as a *new* day in my life—each day was merely a repetition of the last, without any change or hope of change.

At seventeen everything seemed to crowd in upon me. My emotional life had already begun to emerge. What had been mere childish whims were now adult needs. What had been mere petulance before was now real melancholy. I wanted friends, unpitying people of my own age to go about with. It didn't mean that, because I was a cripple and didn't go out, I hadn't the need for the things that made up the everyday lives of other fellows: football, dances, beer parties and girls. A stab of pain shot through my mind when I realized that all the friendly ties that I had formed in my childhood were now broken by the rift that adolescence had wrought between myself and the boys I had played with as a child. It seemed that instead of coming to a better understanding of my own handicap as I got older, I only became troubled and bitter.

Then the final calamity happened. One day when Katriona Delahunt came to visit me, I saw something sparkle brightly on her finger as she placed her hand on the back of a chair that stood in a shaft of sunlight near the kitchen window. I looked again and saw it was a diamond engagement ring. I just stared and stared. A few minutes later she held out her hand with a blush and showed mother the ring, asking her if she liked it. After mother had congratulated her, she turned and showed it to me. I grunted and turned my head away.

"Don't make a sour face," she said to me with one of her special smiles, putting a hand on my shoulder. "I'll still come to see you after I'm married."

She was married some months later on a fine June morning in the University Church. I was brought down by mother in my wheelchair. There was a large crowd of her friends present, but as she and her husband came out of the church, she saw me and a bright smile lit up her darling face. I had no resistance against that.

She was now Katriona Delahunt no longer, but Mrs. Maguire, a very nice name, but it was a long time before I could get used to it. I met Mr. Maguire. He was kind, but I was very jealous.

The months passed. Life at home went on changing. It seemed as if there were now two families in the house, the brothers and sisters I had grown up with, and the ones that came after us. We formed the "older" family, they the "younger" one. Mother still looked almost the same then as she did when I was a child. Perhaps she was a little stouter, and her black hair was slightly streaked with gray, but she had the same smile, the same sparkling blue eyes and lightness of step. She was unconquerable. Father looked rather more aged. His beautiful mop of fair hair had gone and the only remaining signs of it were two tufts on his temples that looked exactly like little balls of gray wool stuck on with paste. Yet he was still as tough as nails, with a pair of hands that were gnarled and hardened by the lifting of concrete blocks and the constant twisting of the trowel. He might bawl at us, but I knew he was rather proud of us all too.

I was an uncle, for already Lily had three children. We teased her by saying she was trying to beat mother's record.

"Keep up the family tradition, Lil!" we would say to her. "Don't let us down!"

But even when I was in the midst of my great family, I felt outside of them, an "odd-man-out." I couldn't reach them, I couldn't enter into the spirit that animated them. They may not have changed in reality, but in my eyes they had become more inaccessible and further beyond my reach. I seemed every day to be drifting farther and farther beyond the orbit of their lives. It was while I was in the very midst of them that I felt more than ever how very far apart I was from them and from all that they worked for and believed in.

On the night of my seventeenth birthday I got up from the sofa where I had been lying and managed to make my way out into the back garden. I was hot and wanted a little air. I crawled over and sat down on a broken piece of plank under a tree. It was June and the air was filled with the scent of flowers. I could hear the least sound, from the twittering and movement of birds in the branches above me to the honking of car horns in the distance. The moonlight made a pattern on the ground in front of me through the waving branches of the stunted old tree I was sitting under. The back window was a square of yellow light, and the sound of loud voices came to my ears from the kitchen within.

It was a beautiful night, calm, gentle, yet alive. The moonlight made everything seem all silver. I almost imagined I heard the noise of the stars as they glimmered in the dark sky.

I sat on the broken bit of board, letting all the calm and peace of the night soak into me. I seemed to be lost in a moonlit dream, away from all the things that made my everyday world such a hell to live in. For a moment I was happy. Then I remembered. The future yawned like a black pit before me. I felt trapped and chained.

What was I, I asked myself as I sat there? Just one of God's practical jokes! My life seemed patternless, without purpose or worth. I was imprisoned within the walls that I now felt closing in around me as I grew up. I longed terribly to be free. I longed passionately to break loose and escape.

9

LOURDES

I HAD BEEN fond of music from an early age. As a child I'd sit by the radio for a long time, listening to whatever kind of music attracted me most. Slowly, I learned to discriminate and decided I liked the type which the rest of the family hated and never listened to—the type which I later found out was called "classical." As I got older I became more attached to it and mother, seeing me sitting rapt, listening to a broadcast of an orchestral concert or some opera, would throw up her eyes and mutter:

"You and your mad music!"

But I only learned something of the real beauty of music when, one day as I was writing upstairs, I heard dimly the strains of a piece of music coming from the wireless downstairs. Immediately I leaped from the bed and half flung myself down the stairs, crawling as fast as I could into the kitchen. There I sat, listening to it in a sort of trance. It was slow, majestic, noble, and to my ears it sounded almost intolerably lovely. It seemed to sink down and touch a chord deep inside me that made my whole soul quiver with a kind of ecstasy. I sat, staring into a world that the music had wrought for me, until the last beautiful strains had faded away. Then I sat silently for a long time, only gradually finding my way back to the ordinary world of every day. It was my first time to hear Handel's *Largo*. It was an unforgettable experience.

Music opened up another new world to me, a bright and beautiful world, at times gay and boisterous, but more often thoughtful and sad. I didn't hear much of it, except over the radio, and I have never seen an opera or been at a symphony concert in my life. But even so, I soon began to know all the great composers and recognize their music. Chopin became my favorite: I could sit listening to his piano music all day if I had the opportunity.

There would often come a feeling, as I sat listening to music, that my life was not so dull and purposeless as I thought it to be: I seemed to see it all laid out carefully, like a vast jigsaw puzzle that was slowly taking shape as the pieces fell one by one into place. I seemed to feel, as I listened, an undercurrent of emotion that made me calm and hopeful, that brought with it a vague promise or message of something to come.

But I only felt like that while the music lasted. It was like getting a breath of air and a glimpse of the sky before the windows were closed again and the door locked. There was nothing for me to do but go back to my pencil and jotter and look on while my brothers and sisters grew up and went their own ways, becoming in my eyes, not brothers and sisters any longer but men and women.

In spite of music, the house was like a prison, enclosing me within its walls. I wanted to fight against this feeling of defeat: I hated to feel I was beaten. But whatever little will power I may have had seemed to be ebbing away from me. I came to dread the thought of having to face another day. Worst of all, I began to feel that there was something stupid, something cruel and senseless behind my affliction. If I thought of God at all, it was only with a sense of resentment. I prayed each night with the others, but I did so automatically, without putting any thought or sincerity behind what I said. Even God seemed to be slipping away from me as I got older.

Then one day Mrs. Maguire came to me and said, "Christy, what about your going to Lourdes?"

All my life I'd heard people talk of it and I felt a strong wish to go there, partly for the adventure of traveling, and partly because, despite my lack of interest in religion, I had the hope deep down inside me, which I hardly dared express even to myself, that a miracle might happen to me.

"Yes," I said. "But . . . what about the money!"

We told mother about it when she came home from shopping and she was delighted. Then we started to make plans. The trip would cost £34. The people organizing the pilgrimage, called the Lourdes Committee, helped me out by giving £10 toward the fare: the next day mother touched my very old aunt for a "fiver." That was as far as we could go.

"Well," said Mrs. Maguire, "I'll get the rest somehow. I'll invite round all my friends and make them play bridge for something tremendous, like five shillings a hundred, and see that they all lose and send you to Lourdes with the proceeds." She smiled her enchanting smile, and I knew it would be all right. It was.

For hours before I left, I was very jittery. This was my first trip abroad, and worse still, I would be traveling alone —or rather without anyone I knew. The thought terrified me. Would the people understand me? How would I get my meals? How would I be dressed and washed and put to bed? Even at eighteen I still had to be fed, dressed, and washed, and father looked after all my natural functions. I was nearly helpless—except for my left foot.

Mother saw me off at the airport with Mrs. Maguire and her husband, who drove me out there. We had to start off at 3 A.M.

I was put on a stretcher and lifted into the plane by two

sturdy ambulance men. As I wasn't exactly a stretcher case, I was put on a seat next to a window, much to my joy. Everything was done so efficiently, and all was so nice and cozy inside the plane that I quite forgot to worry about anything. The doctor was nice, the priest was nice, and the nurses were nice, especially one with dark eyes and fair hair. "Cherry Ripe" I called her.

Soon we were flying out over the Irish Sea, over the coast of Wales, and then across the English Channel. Now I looked at my fellow pilgrims for the first time.

On the seat next to me sat a girl of nineteen, her bright auburn hair framing a pretty face, though one lined with pain. She was smiling with her eyes even though her legs and spine were paralyzed. She had had infantile paralysis from the age of ten and had never walked since. We became friendly, and she told me her name was Marie and that she came from County Wicklow. She talked about books and films and the sister who always went to dances and told her about them afterward. "I'd love to go to a dance, too, sometime," she said, staring dreamily out the window. I thought she seemed happy in spite of everything. But later I heard her sigh wearily and saw her pass a hand across her forehead as if in a gesture of pain. "Please God," she said, "I'll walk again some day. And *then* I'll go to my first dance." She died at Lourdes two days later.

Then there was a little chap from Kerry—Danny somebody—who'd lost the use of both legs as well as his right hand a few weeks before. All he could talk about was the cow he used to milk on the farm. We all made fun of him because he talked with a country brogue, but it didn't bother him, and he went on talking about Nellie, his cow, and how he would milk her again when he got better.

There was the elderly woman in the corner with palsied hands and misshapen feet who prayed all the time. There was the strong young man with a tanned face who was stone blind. There was the smiling little girl, deaf and dumb, clutching her big doll tightly. In front of me squatted Tommy, cheerful, with a pleasant voice. He hadn't any arms or legs. And right behind me lay a young married woman who had contracted tuberculosis after the birth of her first baby a year ago. She lay prone on a stretcher, pale and worn, moaning feebly now and then. A few days before we were due to return to Dublin, she sank into a coma and died, still in great pain.

As I saw all those people, each with his or her own suffering, a new light began to dawn upon me. I was rather bewildered: I had not imagined there could be so much suffering in the world. I had been rather like a snail shut away in his own narrow little shell and that was only now beginning to see the great crowded world that lay beyond. Not only were all those people afflicted but, to my surprise, their handicaps were actually worse than my own! Up to then, I had not thought that was possible. I felt as if I had been blind all along and that only now was I seeing with my eyes and really feeling with my heart the plight of others whose burdens were so great as to make mine seem nothing in comparison.

At last our plane touched down at Tarbes aerodrome and we were in France. I looked out the cabin window. The Pyrenees reared up away in the background. At the aerodrome there were groups of people here and there looking on as we disembarked. These were mostly peasants from the neighboring farms which I had seen from the air, laid out like a huge patchwork quilt.

We were got off the plane at last and placed in an open-air ambulance which took us along long winding roads to the convent where we were to stay during our seven days' pilgrimage. This was in the little town of Lourdes itself.

As our van drew into the square before the convent, I caught my first view of the famous Basilica and beautiful Rosary Square. The long, slender spire with its golden cross rose sheer up into the brilliant blue sky, and from within the depths of the Chapel came the rhythmical chant of a choir singing a hymn to Mary. Already there were large crowds gathered in the Square, some kneeling, some sitting on the seats that were ranged around and reading or dozing in the sun, while others were just walking about taking photographs.

We were lifted from the ambulance, put into chairs like

Chinese rickshaws, and wheeled into the convent. It was now almost noon and outside the sun was blazing down fiercely from a cloudless sky. But in the ward everything was cool and bright. Dinner came soon. A young nurse fed me with a spoon, and I was too hungry to feel any silly embarrassment at this.

We were not brought out to the Grotto that first day, but were advised to rest after our long journey. I was still feeling rather like a new boy amid these strange surroundings and towards night I began to feel very lonely and forgotten. I tried hard to pray, but I kept thinking of home and my parents. I was just about to hide my head under the blankets and give way to tears when the door opened and the night nurse came in. My heart gave a leap—it was Cherry Ripe again, a cluster of golden curls peeping coquettishly from beneath the stiff white nurse's cap she was wearing. She went from bed to bed, making sure we were all comfortable for the night. She arrived at my bed, smiled brightly, and asked if I would like to be tucked in some more.

"Oh, yes," I said quickly, although I was as tucked in as could be.

"There we are," she smiled, as she doubled the edges of the sheets under the mattress and straightened my pillow. "Comfy now?"

"Very," I mumbled. The last thing I remember as I went off to sleep was her smiling as she bent over me to pull the clothes up over my shoulder. I slept soundly that night.

Next morning we were brought down to the famous Healing Baths, where already there were big crowds of various nationalities assembled, all waiting to touch the wonderful waters of the underground spring over which the modern baths were built.

As I waited my turn, I looked about me. There must have been close on three hundred persons gathered in the small forecourt of the low concrete building which housed the baths. Nearly three-quarters of them were in wheelchairs like myself. Some could not sit upright and were forced to lie on their backs the whole time. Others were deprived of whole limbs, while a number went about on crutches, hobbling from place to place with difficulty. I saw them all—legless, armless, sightless, some looking like living corpses as they lay under the newly risen sun. It was like the Court of Miracles in Victor Hugo's novel. Among them all, I felt very small and insignificant.

Now it was my turn to go in to be bathed. I was wheeled in, seated on a wooden bench, and stripped naked by two Frenchmen. All the cubicles in the building were of marble, the "bath" being a deep, square cavity hewn out of the floor itself, with steps leading down to the water. On the wall opposite hung a simple wooden crucifix with prayers inscribed in Latin beneath it.

I was lifted gently by each arm, carried down the steps and then lowered into the water slowly. I gasped as I felt the cold water go over my head. I was raised up quickly, and one of the men asked me in broken English if I wanted to go in again. I nodded, and they lowered me in once more. I heard the two men above me recite prayers in French. They lifted me out and one of them held a small cross to my lips for me to kiss.

It may have been pure fancy, I don't know, but after I had got out of that water I felt as if I was reborn; it was like stepping out from a tomb into the light of day.

That afternoon I saw the Grotto for the first time. Now Lourdes was really packed, and as I was wheeled down the broad road leading to the Shrine, throngs of pilgrims passed me by and the air was filled with a dozen languages: French, Italian, Spanish, Portugese, Swedish, Danish— so many that it was like a mad medley. Yet everyone, whether they came from Dublin or Rome, from Paris or Stockholm, from Milan or Madrid, had one purpose in common that day, to pray and to hope.

When I arrived at the Grotto I could see nothing but a multitude of people kneeling before it with bowed heads. But everything was well organized, and a way was made for the wheelchairs so as to place them near the Shrine.

Soon I was at the altar rails along with the others. I timidly lifted my eyes up and gazed on the marble statue of the tall, beautiful Lady in the blue robe, with the little peasant girl kneeling before her, her hands clasped in ecstasy. From her niche, hewn out of the solid wall of rock Mary gazed serenely down on the vast gathering of her children who now knelt at her feet and gave her their sorrows as well as their love.

I prayed and I prayed that I might be cured.

That night I took part in a torchlight procession through the little town. I shall not easily forget the scene.

From seven in the evening till about eight, thousands had gathered in the Rosary Square, and as dusk descended and shrouded the surrounding hills in a veil of mist, thousands of wax tapers were lit and the procession from the Basilica to the Shrine began, led by the principal Church dignitaries of the countries taking part in the pilgrimage. The entire façade of the beautiful Basilica was illuminated, sparkling vividly against the black velvet of the night sky.

As we wended our way through the little town on the road to the Grotto, the crowd lifted their voices and sang "Ave Maria." The notes rose and fell on the soft night air and echoed back from the near-by hills. Thousands more lined the route, all holding lighted candles, flickering in the gentle breeze.

In contrast, the Grotto itself was in darkness, save for a single candle on the marble altar. The crowd, still singing, knelt in a semicircle round the Shrine, the flames from their candles lighting up the scene and sparkling on the crown of pearls circling the Virgin's head.

It was the most beautiful moment of my life.

I was asleep when we reached Dublin. I awoke when a hand touched my shoulder and shook it slightly.

"We're back home."

I looked up lazily and was about to yawn when I saw it was Cherry Ripe. She was standing in front of me, smiling. Somehow she had heard I painted with my left foot and now asked me if I would paint her a picture when I got home, if I had the time. I nodded my head vigorously, meaning to assure her that I had all the time in the world. She then asked me for my address so that she might call for the painting. I tried to tell her. But all that came out of my mouth was a queer sort of noise. I tried again. I tried again. I got desperate. Then, wildly, I scraped off my left shoe and sock, and, leaning backward, I raised my left foot above my head, plucked the pencil from her breast pocket and wrote my address on the fly-leaf of her prayer book.

Then it was time to go. I looked back as I was being lifted into the ambulance that was to take me home. There she was on the steps of the plane, laughing with one of the crew, a tall handsome chap with fair hair. I hated him.

She hasn't called for the picture yet.

Home. . . . The family was glad to see me after my week's absence. I, too, was glad to see all the old faces again. France was beautiful; Kimmage was home.

I was still feeling rather dazed after all the strange scenes I had witnessed, and all the excitement I had been through. For the past week I had forgotten myself amid the things I'd seen and the people I'd met.

But at home it was different. Here everyone was well and ordinary—except me. My sisters and brothers weren't like the people I'd seen at Lourdes: they could walk, talk, and do all that normal persons can do. When Peter or Paddy talked, the words came clearly, you knew what they were saying. When *I* spoke all that came was strange, jumbled noises. My brothers could use their hands without any trouble, but when I attempted to use mine, they flew this way and that. They were useless to me. They were just lumps of twisted flesh.

After a few days Lourdes became just a memory, and when the magic had worn off I became aware of myself again, aware of the emptiness and boredom of my life. Lourdes was over, and I was the same as before.

I felt as if I were getting back into an old coat again. Everything was the same. I was resenting the old way of living, the old way of thinking. I wanted something to live for, and there was nothing. I wanted my life to have a purpose, a value, but there was none. It was hollow, meaningless. I felt *flat*, searching for something I couldn't find, reaching for something I couldn't grasp.

I knew quite well that, no matter how I might appear on the surface, no matter how I might pretend to others or how much I lied to myself, I would never be happy or at peace with myself as long as I was crippled like this. I remembered Lourdes and the people I had met on the way to the Grotto, and again I tried to be like them—patient, cheerful, resigned to their suffering, knowing the reward that awaited them in the next world. But it was no use. I was too human. There was too much of the man in me and not enough of the humble servant who submits willingly to his Master's will. I wanted to see and to know more of this world before I thought about the next. Despite the wonder and beauty of Lourdes I was still very much the boy who hadn't yet learned how to be meek.

10

THE HOUSE THAT MOTHER BUILT

LOURDES HAD LEFT a lasting impression on my mind. I saw that, far from being alone and isolated as I thought myself to be, I was merely one of a brotherhood of suffering that stretched over the whole globe. I remembered the courage and perseverance that shone in the faces of the afflicted people who came from all parts of the world to hope and pray at the feet of the Virgin in the Grotto. There I had seen the story of my own life reflected in the eyes of those I had prayed with, those men and women who spoke different tongues and who lived according to different ideals, but who were now made all brothers and sisters, all part of one family by right of a common heritage of pain. No one thought of anyone else as a "foreigner" in that holy little village; all the barriers that separate single persons and whole nations from one another were broken down and burned away by that common need for understanding and communication which we all felt and which suffering alone could have inspired.

Yet here I was at home again, away from all the splendor and glory of Lourdes and from all the things that had made me forget myself in that first rush of sympathy and communion with others. Here I was surrounded, not by a great multitude of the afflicted, but by my family, strong, healthy, normal individuals who, though unconsciously, made me feel rather like a puppet in contrast. Like a bird that had been set free for a while, I felt as if I were about to be locked in my cage again.

A week or so after my return the awful sense of loneliness began to creep in upon me again and play havoc with my thoughts. I tried to lose myself in reading, and Mrs. Maguire gave me lots of books. But I would read no one but Dickens, and he only made me sad, even if he did make me laugh now and then.

Mother saw that I was disappointed, and that, more and more as time went on, I was thinking and brooding about the things that "might have been" in my life, thinking more bitterly about them now because I had begun to feel their need and know the loss of them. Though we still understood one another, she couldn't try to comfort me with words now or laugh away my little moods of sadness. Even between us two, mother and me, there seemed to be a barrier, a new kind of glass wall that wouldn't let us reach one another. I was feeling things and wanting things that even mother only vaguely comprehended.

One Thursday evening, about seven or eight days after my return from Lourdes, I was sitting at my window gazing gloomily out into the gathering autumn dusk that was slowly covering the street outside in a dark purple haze. In the kitchen behind me I could hear the sausages frizzling in the pan as mother got the dinner ready with all the children chattering and crowding around her. Mona stood before the mirror, painting her lips and powdering her nose, preparing for a dance as usual, while Peter, look-ing very pleased with himself, polished his shoes vigorously with an old woolen rag and gave me an enormous wink, a sure sign that he had a "date" on.

Suddenly, from out the corner of my eye, I saw the headlights of a car piercing the deepening twilight as it came round the bend in the road opposite. It disappeared behind some bushes but in a second came in sight again and stopped outside our door. A man stepped out, paused to peer uncertainly at the number of the house, then, ap-parently satisfied, opened the front gate and came up the steps.

"Here's someone," I grumbled.

"Who is it?" inquired Peter noticing the parked car.

"See," I told him gruffly.

Hearing the knock, mother went to the door to answer it. I heard her speaking to someone at the hall door, and a moment later she came back into the kitchen with the strange man.

"This is Christy," she told him as they entered.

I looked up at him as he stood before me, smiling down at me. I saw he was a well-built man with gray-green eyes, eyes that, while they looked at me, seemed at the same time to look *into* me.

He sat down on a chair close by and told me he was a doctor who had seen me before as a baby and later at a film show organized for some charity, where he'd seen me on the back of my brother. Somehow he hadn't forgotten me, and had started to look for me a few days ago.

Then he got up, paced up and down thoughtfully for a few moments, and finally sat down on the edge of the table, his arms folded. He began to speak.

"Christy," he said in his deep, pleasant voice, "there is a new treatment for cerebral palsy—the thing that is wrong with you. I believe you can be cured—but only if you are willing to try hard enough with us. I can't help you if you don't try to help yourself. You must *want* to get better before anything can be done for you." Then he leaned forward, his eyes steady on me, "Will you try if I help?" he asked me.

"Will I try!" I thought.

I couldn't speak, so I couldn't answer him. I could only stare. But he must have read the message in my eyes, for he stood up, satisfied, came over to me, put his arm round my shoulders and said:

"Right! We'll start tomorrow."

He said he would send out one of his assistants the next day to examine me and devise a special line of treatment for me, as the method was to treat each patient individually rather than in the mass. I would be treated at home, since they hadn't as yet formed a special clinic of their own.

He stood up to go, but just as he was going out the door, he paused and turned round.

"By the way," he said to me with a slow smile, "my name's Dr. Collis. I'll be seeing you soon." With that he left.

As the door closed upon him, I turned and looked at the faces around me. They were all lit up with happiness and excitement. Father was so overjoyed that his hand trembled as he poured me out a cup of tea.

Mona had forgotten all about her dance and was smiling at me while she absently tore her powder puff to shreds in her hand. Peter, good old Peter, put two spoonfuls of salt instead of sugar into his tea.

But it was at mother that I looked most of all. Like myself, she didn't easily show what she was feeling at any time, but there was a quiet air of joy about her, a subdued glow of happiness in her face that meant more to me than if she had thrown her arms about my neck and wept with thanksgiving.

And I—what did I feel at that moment of my life, the moment I had so longed for and dreamed about ever since I had begun to feel and dream? For a while I didn't feel or think of anything. All my senses were numbed and my brain was dizzy. I couldn't grasp, I couldn't believe the idea that I was to be cured at last. It was too much for me. It staggered me.

I listened to all the others talking excitedly around me at the tea table in a sort of dream trance. I couldn't distinguish a word. I sipped my tea absently each time father lifted the cup to my lips and ate my bread without tasting it.

It was later, as I sat round the fire with mother and father when the rest had gone out to enjoy themselves after tea, that I started to think about the news I had heard that day, and only then did the reality and truth of it come to my mind. I don't think I was excited in the ordinary ways about it as the rest of the family had been —I just wondered at the strangeness and the queer beauty of it all.

I had gone to Lourdes, joyful and full of hope—almost of confidence, I'm afraid. A week later I had come home, a little shaken and maybe a little wiser, but very disappointed. Everything had seemed just as it was before. My heart had been light and trustful at the thought of visiting Lourdes. It was dull and heavy when I came home, because I knew that, no matter how much I longed to change it, my life would always be the same: drab, empty, and colorless.

Then, even while I was still thinking bitterly about it that very day, a doctor had suddenly come in and told me that I could be cured! In a very few words he had changed the pattern of my whole life, he had given the past some significance and the future some promise, some definite purpose; he had given me something to fasten my thoughts and aspirations on to, something to live for, work for, and fight for at the moment when I was sure that there was nothing but empty and fruitless years before me.

It may have been mere chance, mere coincidence, but to me, because of all it meant and brought to me later, it then seemed, and has seemed since, nothing less than a miracle—a beautiful little miracle, not because of all the good it brought me, but because it created faith where before there had been only bitterness and disillusion. It showed me that in the great Plan of life we all matter, even the least of us, because we are all a part of it, and even the small unknown ones are very important because they help to hold the big ones together lest they tumble.

I saw in that first flash of understanding that I, too, had a part to play, no matter how small it was.

That night, before I went to sleep, I prayed a prayer of thankfulness—and repentance for having doubted.

The doctor who came out next day to examine me was a young man, tall, handsome, with a certain military bearing that impressed even while it subdued me a little. He was slow and deliberate in his movements and his whole manner suggested an easy confidence that communicated itself to those about him. I felt myself liking him at once. His name was Louis Warnants, a name which I shall always remember with gratitude and affection.

Dr. Warnants drew up a special line of treatment that consisted mostly in certain physical exercises which I could carry out myself at home, with perhaps a little help from the family if I wanted it. This, he told me, was only a preliminary test. If he saw that I was responding, no matter how slightly, to it, he would then put me to a much harder routine of exercises which would become more involved and intricate as I got on. I found out that the exercises were called physiotherapy, which I thought was a perfect giant of a name.

After that Dr. Warnants came to me once a week—every Sunday in fact. Each time he came, he made me go through the exercises while he looked on, taking careful note of the ones I found most difficult to do and pointing out to me where I went wrong.

It was rather funny the way everyone at home used to rush about and fall over themselves every Sunday afternoon when the hour approached for Dr. Warnants to come. I think they were all a little in awe of him, perhaps even a little apprehensive, for, although he was a very nice gentleman and his manners impeccable, there were no half measures about him: he took his job seriously and placed it above everything else.

One Sunday afternoon when he came to treat me a little earlier than usual, the kitchen was full with all my sisters and brothers, both big and small. In next to no time, mother got rid of the younger ones by rushing them all upstairs, but then didn't quite know what to do with the older ones. Dr. Warnants solved the problem.

"Good afternoon, everyone," he said politely, looking around at the six or seven that were still left. "You've got rid of all the lambs, Mrs. Brown, I see. But the sheep are still left."

Then he went over to where Jim was sitting.

"Hello, you're Jim, aren't you?" he said, smiling genially, "It's a topping day for a walk. Allow me to help you on with your coat."

The others took the hint and departed in perfect good humor, Dr. Warnants acting as doorman.

It was very difficult for Dr. Warnants to treat me in the house because the only room available was the kitchen itself, and that was much too small and awkward. During exercises, when I stretched out my leg, it would bang against the fire grate, and when I turned round on my stomach, my head would be under a chair and my legs beneath the table, so that each time I lifted my head I'd get a resounding smack on it.

"Either you're too big, Christy, or this room's too small," he said.

"I think it's a mixture of both, doctor," mother said.

"If only we had a little more space," said Dr. Warnants with a sigh as I banged my head again for the third or fourth time that afternoon.

At the back of the house there was a good bit of waste ground which everybody at home had tried to cultivate, but in vain. True, they had actually succeeded in planting and raising cabbage and turnips and some potatoes there once in a while, but they all seemed to wither and die after a time. It made no difference whether they put vegetables or flowers into it, the old bit of land stubbornly refused to be cultivated. It seemed to want to remain a wilderness.

But mother was determined that it would not. Frequently she offered half a crown to any one of us who'd make the best attempt to do something with it.

Now, however, she had an idea—a sudden brain wave. Why not make use of the back garden in another way? It would help both Dr. Warnants and myself greatly if we had a room to ourselves away from the noise and disturbance of the house. So, mother thought, why not build that room on the ground at the back where we'd be away from everything? Ah, but the money—there's always the question of money! She hadn't an idea what it would cost, but as she lived in a family of bricklayers, she was slowly able to estimate what the cost of the building materials would be by making unobtrusive little inquiries among father and the boys. She found it would be a cool £50.

Still, she would not let this defeat her. She was determined to put her ambitious notion into practice. So she plunged straightway into the thing—borrowing, selling, joining money clubs, visiting the good old pawnshop, looking up some well-to-do old uncles and aunts, after discovering they weren't all dead after all. For weeks she carried on this secret cash gathering unknown to any of the family except me. I gave her my moral support throughout the campaign, of course.

When she had netted about £20, she decided to make a start. She knew it was useless putting the matter to father, for he'd oppose it on the grounds that the "Authorities," a favorite word of his, wouldn't allow it because the house we were living in was subject to certain rules of a body of people known as the City Corporation.

But she put the idea to her four bricklayer sons. None of them was enthusiastic. They all would be willing enough if one of them would make a start, but as usual in such cases, no one was ready to make such a start.

Mother was so made that she must always put her ideas to the test at once. She decided to take matters into her own hands and start immediately herself. She went out one afternoon and ordered a hundred concrete blocks, four bags of cement, and two bags of mortar. "For a start," she said!

The stuff arrived the same day. Poor father almost collapsed when he came home from work that evening and saw all the blocks piled up neatly in the front garden. He stood swaying, holding on to the gate. His mouth opened, but he didn't seem to be able to speak as he gazed at the pile. He staggered up the front walk, opened the door, and said in a sort of hoarse whisper to mother, "What's the idea?"

"Oh, I forgot to tell you," said mother casually as she put his dinner on the table. "I'm going to build a house for Christy in the back garden."

"My God!" said father, staring at her. "Do you want us all to be evicted? Do you realize what you're doing? The authorities will—"

"Yes, yes, I know all that," said mother quietly. "But do take your dinner now, like a good man, or it'll be cold on you."

"Only over my dead body," father said, his mouth full of stew.

"I'd bury your body first, of course," mother replied ever so meekly.

Seeing that it was useless to argue the thing out with her, father next resorted to a plan of non-cooperation, saying that he wouldn't set one block and that he'd advise the four other bricklayers in the house to have nothing to do with the business either.

For a moment I thought mother was beaten. But she just smiled and said:

"Very well, if none of you will do it, I'll build it myself."

They all laughed at that—the idea of a woman building a house!

Next day mother rose particularly early, got breakfast ready very fast, sent the six younger children off to school, and got through all the household work during the morning so that she could have the whole afternoon free. Lunchtime came and went as usual. Mother didn't say a word of what was in her head to anyone.

At about four o'clock that afternoon I suddenly noticed that mother was spending a lot of time in the back of the house. Then I became aware of peculiar sounds coming from the back garden. Very curious, I managed to stumble to the pantry window. I looked out.

There was mother, on her knees on the grass, a bucket of cement on one side of her and a jug of water on the other. She held a trowel in her right hand. She was looking proudly at the line of blocks she had already set out before her!

That evening when she had served dinner and tea, she went quietly back to her work in the back garden. A few minutes later, father, happening to go into the yard for something, saw her. He stood stock still, then slowly he approached the growing wall. He touched it with his foot. "What's this?" he asked. "What do you think you're doing?"

Mother looked up. "I'm building Christy's house," she said, setting in another block.

Father said nothing for a minute or so, he just watched. Then he looked a bit closer. Then his hand went out; he pulled it back. He walked to the other end of the line of blocks. His upper lip twitched a bit, he paused. . . . At last he said, "Look-it! You're doing it all wrong, woman. Where's your foundation?"

"I knew I was forgetting something," mother answered rather crossly.

By this time the other four bricklayers had come out and gathered round.

"Look-it, boys," said father, turning to them. "Your mother's trying to do *our* work!"

"Terrible," said Paddy, looking critically at the row of cement blocks and shaking his head disapprovingly. "You haven't even got them level, mother!"

"That's women for you," said Peter, "always trying to be like men. Go back to your dishes, ma."

"Well, if it's a man's job, get on with it," she said. She just stood up and wiped her hands on her apron. Slowly she turned and left them. As she passed me she smiled.

The five bricklayers stood and looked at each other.

"C'mon," said father as mother disappeared into the house. "Let's start."

So they built my little house in the back garden. The work went through many vicissitudes and it looked at one time as though it would never be finished. The thing that held us up most of all was money. Mother's £20 had been used up quickly and we seemed to come to a standstill.

Father asked me one day what it looked like with only the four walls built and concrete foundation put in.

"Like an unfinished symphony," I said.

Then mother managed to scrape together another few pounds and the work was resumed. They appointed me foreman over them, and from time to time I pointed out to them what way I'd like certain parts of it built and where I wanted the fireplace, the window, and the door. There were many debates between father and the four boys on technical points which I didn't understand, though I'd try to look very learned as I listened to them.

After some months the roof was put on and the ceiling backed up. Then the funds ran low again and Operation House ceased.

Later things brightened up. They got to work on the floor and hearthstone, and next they put in the window frames and the door. The chimney was already up, of course, so that at least we could have a fire in it, if nothing else!

Slowly, by degrees, the place began to take shape: the window panes were in, the walls were plastered, and even a wooden skirting ran around the floor. As far as the actual building of it was concerned, it was finished.

But it still looked rather like a vault, without any human touch about it. It only needed some bits of furniture now to make it alive.

Piece by piece the furniture moved in—a divan, a bed, a few chairs, and a table. Then my brother-in-law, a sawyer, made me a handsome little bureau in which to hold some odds and ends. The lino was put down, the wallpaper put up, and the curtains hung. In a few days more, the electric light was installed and the door and window frames painted. It was ready to be lived in at last.

It was originally intended only to make a sort of exercise-room of it, a gymnasium where Dr. Warnants might treat me undisturbed. As time went on, however, I slowly converted it into both a living room and study, where I ate, read, wrote, and slept. I got them to put up bookshelves for me which gradually filled up one by one.

Thus, at last, I had really broken away from the family,

from the noise and busy life of the house. Now at last I could live in comfortable solitude and paint and write as much as I liked in perfect freedom without the constant drumming of voices in my ears. In summer, I could sit by the open window and read, the only sound being the happy chorus of the birds in the trees outside, and when the winter came it was even more pleasant, for then I'd sit by the fire in the dark and watch the red glow dance on the walls and fall on the backs of books on the shelves, making their gilt lettering stand out in the gloom.

My reading was still rather small, my chief companion being Charles Dickens. I read six or seven of his books in very quick succession, my special favorite being *David Copperfield,* which I read three times with an unabated eagerness. The book which thrilled me most of all was *Captain Cook's Voyages,* which I got at Christmas from Mrs. Maguire. I remember the wonder and excitement I felt as I read of lost islands and shipwrecks and bands of bloodthirsty savages whooping on the sands as the helpless ship floundered on the rocks.

It made me dream of traveling some day to the great cities of the world and meeting people and seeing strange sights. My imagination was busy conjuring up mental pictures of ruined cities, silent and dead, of steaming wet jungles full of life, and of vast trackless deserts, eternities of yellow sand bathed in pitiless sunlight.

It was great fun, going off on those travels of imagination through the pages of books. My reading, small and narrow though it was as yet, helped me to know something of a world beyond the four walls of my study.

Meanwhile, my treatment went on under Dr. Warnants. We were able to make better headway now that we had more space to move in. It was still very crude, this treatment for cerebral palsy—as the causes of it were as yet essentially unknown and, therefore, the treatment of the complaint was still in the embryo stage.

Then, one day. Dr. Collis came to me and told me that he had decided to send me over to London to see his sister-in-law Mrs. Eirene Collis, who was a well-known specialist in cerebral palsy. He wanted to get her opinion as to whether I was likely to respond to treatment before starting me on a full-scale rehabilitation program. He would ask her to examine me herself in the Middlesex Hospital and give him her opinion on my chances of leading a normal life.

I would travel to London by air in a few days' time, and Dr. Warnants, who had gone over ahead of me, would meet me at Northolt Airport and drive me to the hospital to see Mrs. Collis. Mother was to travel with me.

I realized then that everything depended on Mrs. Collis' verdict—that my future really lay in her hands. If she decided I was too far advanced a case to benefit from treatment, then I would be back where I was before Dr. Collis found me, back to the old life of inactivity and hopelessness again.

If, on the other hand, she should conclude that I would respond favorably to treatment, then my life would have some meaning, some ultimate worth and value. Then I could begin to break down some of the walls that stood between me and an ordinary existence.

I was at the crossroads.

11

FLYING VISIT

IT WAS JANUARY, 1949, the start of the new year, when I made the flight to London with mother to see Mrs. Collis for her verdict. We stayed just one day. That was all. Yet even in the space of a few hours my entire life was changed.

We all expected mother to be excited, and indeed a little nervous, for this was to be her first air trip.

"You'd better bring your prayer book along with you," I jibed. "St. Peter is bound to let you in then."

But we didn't know her half enough at all. She took the prospect of flying quite calmly.

"Might as well die in the air as on the ground," she summed it up. Next day she went out and bought a new hat.

"This is for London," she announced, trying it on before the mirror. "Got it in Clery's. Do you like it?"

Father looked at it from right angles, left angles, and a host of other angles, paused, looked very critical, paused again, scratched his head, and spoke.

"Hmm . . . not bad, mind you, very—er—artistic. But, tell me, what's it supposed to be?"

It was a tiny black satin thing with a huge plumage of feathers and a dark veil.

"Too bright," Peter chimed in. "People will start calling you Mrs. Peacock."

In spite of this, mother wore her new hat the day we flew to London, and smiled triumphantly when Dr. Collis told her he liked it.

I thought by now I was a veteran at air travel, but I became violently airsick during the crossing and for a few minutes thought I was about to die. Then the hostess stopped by me and asked if I would like the special tablets for airsickness; she said she had some in her handbag.

I looked up and my awful headache immediately vanished. I didn't need the tablets, for I forgot how sick I felt when she felt my pulse. She was a wonderful hostess. . . .

We arrived at Northolt at eleven o'clock on a bright, cold Saturday morning. Dr. Warnants was there to meet us and hoisted me across his shoulder and into a waiting taxi. I didn't like this mode of traveling on a person's back, for I thought it rather undignified and it made me feel foolish. I would much rather have crawled to the taxi.

We set out on the drive to Middlesex Hospital. I looked out of the window as the car wound its way through the London traffic, seeing the big jostling crowds outside the huge shopwindows, the ceaseless stream of red buses and motorcars and cyclists, all seeming to be converging into one mass of noise and motion. I saw the tall gray buildings outlined against the smoke-blue sky. Over all rose the sounds that issue from the heart of a great city every moment of the day.

Soon I saw a patch of vivid green in the background which, as we came closer, I saw was a park with beautiful trees lining its sides.

"Regents Park," explained Dr. Warnants, as we were passing it.

It made me think of the old Phoenix Park in Dublin and of the happy times I had as a child with my brothers down in the green meadows of Donnelly's Hollow, so many years ago, a happy child living in a bright world of his own —and here I was, at eighteen, moving through the wide streets of London on my way to a momentous meeting. I was silent and just sat staring out of the taxi window because I knew that, in a short time, I would find out what course my future was to follow. I was anxious to know, yet frightened to find out, because it would have such enormous effect on my life. It would be either the summit or the pit.

Finally, the car pulled up outside a huge stone building with a great many steps leading up to it. This was the Middlesex Hospital, my destination. We were taken up in a lift to a little consulting room to await the arrival of Mrs. Collis. Dr. Warnants smiled as he helped me into a chair.

"Scared?" he asked me, fingering a little brass statue on the mantelshelf.

I shook my head just to give myself courage.

"You are, you know," he continued, looking at me. "You're scared stiff, but you're too stubborn to admit it even to yourself. That's good."

Mother was perfect, she just sat calmly looking through some magazines that were on the table, munching some ham sandwiches she had brought along with her. This was the first time she had ever been outside Dublin, and yet she seemed as calm and cheerful as if she had been at home in the kitchen, cutting bread for the children's tea.

But, though she did not show it, I knew very well that inwardly she was feeling and thinking the same things as myself: that she understood almost as well as I did, what this interview would mean to me and how my whole life would be ruled according to its result, and, without as much as speaking one word of help, she gave me a part of her own courage and strength to face up to it.

Suddenly the door behind me opened. I looked round and I saw that a man and woman had come into the room. At once my eyes were drawn towards the small, thin woman with graying hair, handsome face, and light, springy step. I felt sure that this was Mrs. Collis, and in her presence my doubts and apprehensions soon vanished, because there was something about her—her slow smile, her complete naturalness and casual manner—that made me feel secure and self-possessed, no matter what her verdict might turn out to be.

"Sorry I'm late," she said to us, sitting on the edge of the desk and lighting a cigarette. For a few moments she took no notice of me and just sat chatting about things like the weather, the cost of cigarettes, and Mr. Churchill. Then she tapped her cigarette, slid off the desk and strolled over to me.

"I was just letting some of your tension escape, Christy," she said smiling. "How old are you now?" she asked me, and when mother attempted to tell her my age, she held up her hand and said politely: "Let Christy tell me himself—just for fun."

I managed to grunt that I was eighteen.

"Eighteen?" said Mrs. Collis. "Eighteen years a cripple is quite enough for anyone. Don't you think it's time you did something about it?" I nodded my head in agreement. "Yes, so do I!" she said. "Well then, let's see if we can make anything of you."

Then she called over the man she had come in with. He was young, small sized, with sandy hair and a thin pleasant face.

"This is Mr. Gallagher," said Mrs. Collis as he came over, "one of our staff."

Afterwards we were to become very good friends, Mr. Gallagher and I. He helped a great deal in my struggle, and his name, to me, will always be synonymous with friendliness and understanding.

I was stripped and put lying on the couch while Mrs. Collis examined me, helped by Dr. Warnants and Mr. Gallagher. I didn't understand what they were talking about most of the time. I caught words like cerebrum, basal ganglia, inco-ordination, and many other mystic-sounding words which were perfectly unintelligible to my ear. Mrs. Collis had mother explain to her the main details of my medical history while she examined me.

When the examination was over, Mr. Gallagher helped me on with my clothes again. After that the four of them —Mrs. Collis, Dr. Warnants, Mr. Gallagher and mother —withdrew to the farther corner of the room to speak among themselves for a while. I sat alone on the couch, my heart beating quickly, waiting desperately for the verdict. I sweated all over. It was as if I were on trial for my life.

At last Mrs. Collis came across the room slowly and sat down on the couch beside me.

"Well, Christy," she said. "You haven't come to London in vain. I can find no reason why you shouldn't be cured eventually."

My heart gave a leap of pure joy. I was to be cured! What else mattered now? All the old bitterness and heartache was changed now into an all-pervading happiness that lit up my face and made my heart dance wildly. It was to be the summit after all!

"Yes," continued Mrs. Collis. "You can be cured if you are prepared to do lots of really hard work over the next few years. But—" here she paused, looked steadily at me, and went on—"you must first make a big sacrifice. Nothing good is ever obtained without one, and yours is—you must resolve never to use your left foot again."

My left foot! But that meant everything to me—I could speak only with that, create only with that! It was my only means of communication with the outside world, my only way of reaching the minds of other people and making myself articulate and intelligible. The rest of me was useless, worthless, and that one limb, my left foot, was the only workable thing in my whole body. Without it I would be lost, silent, powerless.

"Yes, I know it's tough," she said, interpreting my thoughts. "It's a tremendous sacrifice. But it's the only way out—there are no short cuts. If you continue to use your left foot you may one day become a great artist or writer with it—but you'll never be cured. You'll never walk, talk, or use your hands, and without being able to do these things you cannot lead a normal life in any sort of society. So, it all simmers down to this—will you promise never to use your left foot again?"

I saw the wisdom of what she had said. There were, indeed, to be no half measures. It was going to be an all-out battle from now on and, if I wanted to win it, I must put everything I had into it—I must pay a big price, perhaps even a cruel price, to win a bigger gain. It would be frightful, but it might bring victory in the end.

"I will," I said to Mrs. Collis—and it was the clearest word I had ever uttered.

She took my hand and pressed it, her eyes alight. "Good boy. It's not going to be easy. You must put your whole mind behind the work we're going to give you, and even then it will be slow, terribly slow, especially at your age. But the first step has been taken—the rest is up to you."

Mrs. Collis explained it to me later. She told me that, although the use of my foot was good for me mentally since it had provided an outlet for my imprisoned mind to express itself, it was bad for me physically, because the use of it imposed a great strain upon the rest of my body, so that, even while it was releasing some of my mental tension, it was making worse the condition of my already crippled muscles. As long as I could make myself understood by using my left foot, I would never think of trying to use my hands. But if I could no longer use my foot, I would then have to concentrate on making some use of the rest of my body.

All very logical, I thought. Nothing could be more true and so full of sense. But there was such a big difference between the word and the action, such a difference between *thinking* about those things and actually carrying them through! It wasn't just a question of tightening my shoelace and tying up my poor old left foot. It went far deeper than that. I felt as if I were about to lock myself up and throw away the key.

Still, what could I do but make the deal? If I were too cowardly to do so, then the past would come rushing back upon me with all its bitterness and black pessimism, as dark and sunless as a winter sky. If I took the chance and "cut off" my left foot, as it were, then I'd enter into a new life, a complete new mode of thinking and acting, and that in itself would be something worth any sacrifice.

We flew back to Dublin that night and were met at the airport by Dr. Collis who drove us home in his car. It seemed that Mrs. Collis had already got in touch with him by phone and he was very delighted with her good news. He told me that he had recently succeeded in forming a Cerebral Palsy Clinic in Merrion Street, Dublin, and the Knights of Malta and the St. John Ambulance Brigade had agreed to provide transport to bring the crippled children to and from the Clinic for treatment from nine in the morning to twelve noon. I was to start attending it on the following Monday morning when the Brigade ambulance would call to collect me.

"There's nothing you can't conquer, Christy," said he to me, putting his hand on my shoulder. "And remember I'm with you all the way."

But I knew then that my first task was to conquer myself, and that the real battle was only beginning.

12

WHAT MIGHT HAVE BEEN

I WAS VERY excited at the prospect of going to the Clinic for the first time. I hadn't the least idea of what it would look like. I imagined cool marble walls, white-coated people and the constant smell of disinfectant.

On the memorable Monday morning, the St. John's ambulance pulled up outside our door at about nine-thirty. I glanced at it from the window apprehensively. I had always thought of ambulances as in some way connected with funerals—somber, spirit-chilling things, full of bleeding bodies.

However, the driver was a cheerful, smiling man who helped father to lift me. That made me a little less afraid. As I sat down on the seat I looked about at my fellow-patients. I saw that I was very much the oldest amongst them. On the stretcher before me lay a small child, not more than a baby, with stiff arms and bent, crooked legs, and a head that lay at a queer angle to the rest of his body. Beside him sat a little girl with bright golden hair and very large eyes. She was very pretty, but her legs were thin and misshapen with protruding bones, and her restless, shaking hands were like my own, but smaller and more fragile. She kept smiling the whole time, and trying to brush her fair ringlets out of her eyes. On the seat next to me a little child lay, completely inert, with set, frozen features that were expressionless but for her eyes, which moved restlessly, inquiringly around. Those two eyes were the only living things about her—they were like the lighted windows of a dead house.

At last the ambulance drew into Merrion Street and came to a stop outside a big stone-gray building.

I looked out of the window. It was a long wide thoroughfare with impressive buildings on each side of it. It rang with an almost constant buzz of traffic. Everyone walking along it seemed to be very businesslike, as if they were all going to important conferences. This wasn't so unnatural as it seemed, for I found out later that on the opposite side of the street were the Government Buildings, where the complicated business of running the whole nation was carried on.

I turned and caught sight of Dr. Warnants coming down the steps of the building which we had stopped outside. I felt reassured when I saw him again.

I couldn't walk, and as far as I could see there was no

sign of any car or chair to wheel me into the building. I looked at Dr. Warnants, and he looked back at me.

"I'll have to do the strong-man act again, old boy," he said with a shrug of his shoulders.

Then he gripped me round the legs and threw me over his back. As he carried me up the steps I saw a little gold plaque on the wall on which was inscribed:

"Dublin Orthopaedic Hospital."

That sounds bad, I said to myself. I wonder what that awfully big word means anyway?

From my position over Dr. Warnants' shoulder I couldn't see my surroundings very well, but from a constant view of the floor and the lower parts of the walls, I knew that we were passing right through the building. We went down a flight of stairs, walked along a corridor in semidarkness for a while, opened a rickety old door at the end, and came out into daylight again.

"That's one journey," said Dr. Warnants between pants. "Now for the other."

I could see we were in some kind of field or other, for there was grass on either side of the gravel path I was being carried over, and by lifting my head from its downward angle, I could glimpse trees all around us. But I was not exactly in the mood to admire the scenery. I was not even in a position to do so, for I could feel the breakfast I had eaten an hour ago coming up my throat again at every step Dr. Warnants took. I had to hold my throat shut to keep it back.

"There the Rugged Path ends, Christy—for the time being!" Dr. Warnants said with a gasp.

I managed to twist my head around and got a view of a long, narrow wooden building, single storied, which looked like a gymnasium hut. As we approached it, I heard sounds of children's voices, both laughing and crying —the majority seemed to be screaming.

The doctor pushed open the door and went in, still carrying me over his shoulder. The moment we entered the full force of the noise hit me with an almost physical sensation. The din was terrific. Children were crying, roaring, screaming, banging toys and anything they could find against the walls and floor, kicking their legs in the air, stamping their feet, crawling and wriggling like crabs over one another. It was awful. I looked about me as Dr. Warnants dumped me on the floor and wondered if I had been taken to the wrong place, for I saw that there was not one child there over three years of age at the most. I thought it must be some kind of nursery or creche. I discovered that the only other adult in the room besides Dr. Warnants and myself was a young man whom I recognized as Mr. Gallagher. He smiled when he saw me—and I thought he was a very brave man after that.

"No treatment this morning, Christy," said Dr. Warnants with a smile as he went by me, carrying two babies in his arms to the other end of the room. "Just relax and look on."

And yet it was a treatment in itself, just looking on. It was an instruction, an education in human suffering, a new, rather frightening experience for one who, until lately, had never seen life beyond the walls of his own home. In the light of this altogether new aspect of life which now lay before me, the things I had seen at Lourdes were only a shadow. This was the substance, the fulfillment of a foreboding. The afflicted people I had met at the Grotto in Lourdes were all adults, all grown men and women, some in great pain, of course, with nothing but wrecked lives behind or before them, but still quite capable of understanding their own affliction or at least becoming resigned to it. But here was no such thing—here there was no reasoning, only helplessness, helplessness and near-horror in the form of twisting, twining babies with crooked little limbs, misshapen heads, distorted features, some lying huddled on the floor, inert and motionless, like empty sacks thrown carelessly here and there around the room. Others were convulsed with wild, endless movement, movement that shook their small bodies as if an electric current were constantly passing through them, making them shake, wriggle and jerk in endless writhings, their little hands clenched, their legs bent and locked together as if in a vise, their heads awry. Suddenly, I realized for the first time what I myself had looked like as a child.

I could easily have pitied them, so young, so helpless and afraid, so entirely dependent upon others, but I did not, for I remembered how bitterly a look of pity had hurt me once. Instead of pity, I began to feel a sympathy, an affinity with those children, a link that enabled me to see and to *feel* the real personalities which lay behind the grotesquely working faces and tense taut limbs, a kind of brotherly insight that let me see beyond the twisted muscle and bone to the imprisoned minds that lay inside. I saw that I was not the only one who was shut away behind prison bars.

When I got home that day all the family crowded round me, wanting to know what the Clinic was like. But I could say nothing. I had seen something and felt something that no words of mine could describe.

After about a week at the Clinic, during which time, as Dr. Warnants put it, I was being "conditioned," I was slowly initiated into the mode of treatment. I found that it was similar to that which I had been receiving at home, except, of course, that it was on a much broader, more organized scale. The exercises at the Clinic were more detailed, more intricate—and a lot more arduous to perform. At first, to be quite truthful, I felt rather silly while doing them. I felt I was a ridiculous sight, sitting among a roomful of kids, a bit silly having to go through the same exercises as they—in fact, I felt like an elephant among a lot of kittens, and I was sure that was how I looked too.

Often, as I pulled myself along on my stomach in among the children—this was all part of the exercises for I wasn't allowed to move about on my behind as I used to do—I'd stop suddenly, as though becoming aware of my surroundings for the first time, look slowly around at all the twisting and inert forms lying about me on the floor, at the faces of Dr. Warnants and Mr. Gallagher as they bent over the children, at the ceiling with its knotted brown beams, at the wooden walls with their high windows through which I caught glimpses of blue sky and white cloud and the green foliage of the trees in the garden outside—I'd see all these things, and quite suddenly I'd pause and ask myself:

"What am I, Christy Brown, doing here? What does all this mean to me—this strange place called a clinic, those two doctors going about in their shirtsleeves, those crippled children with their funny twisted bodies and lolling heads—what have I to do with all this? Why am I here, in this place, instead of writing in the bedroom at home?"

Yes, it was true: I still hadn't become accustomed to the outside world. I still couldn't grasp the reality of it all—the fact that I was now a part of this strange and bewildering, this new and fast-moving world of people and places. I was like a caveman, shut away for years in the darkness and confinement of his own narrow quarters, and now suddenly thrust upon the vast teeming world, gazing blankly, as if seeing the light of day for the first time and being blinded by all that it revealed to him.

Many times, as I sat hunched on the floor staring unseeingly before me, I'd feel a toe nudging me from behind. I'd start and look around, and there'd be Dr. Warnants, standing above me and smiling.

"Daydreaming again!" he'd say to me. "Thinking of all the books you're going to write some day, eh? Snap out of it, old boy! There's a job to be done, you know."

Yes, I knew there *was* a job to be done, and quite a job too. A job that wouldn't be done in a year, two years, or even five years—a job, in fact, that would take a lifetime. I knew that quite well. And yet I couldn't help stopping and thinking of all that had happened to me before I realized that such a job *could* be done. I couldn't help thinking now and then of the old days—not the *good* old days to me, but rather the grim old days, the days when I had nothing to hope for or live for, nothing to dull the pain of the immediate present or to brighten the darkness of the distant future, nothing, in fact, but the pain and inner anguish that grew with the growing awareness of myself and the affliction that I couldn't understand and hated.

It was true—I hated my own affliction, I despised it. I was tormented, revolted at the very thought that I had been made different—cruelly different—from other people. And yet I was soon to realize that it was this very affliction, which I regarded in my worst moments as a curse from God, that was to bring a strange beauty into my life.

I had been attending the Clinic for about a year when it happened. It was a fine spring morning in April and the Clinic had just begun to close for another day. The ambulance men had taken the children out to the waiting car and I was the last one left. I was sitting in a rickety old wheelchair that they used at the Clinic to cart me around in. I was outside the door, enjoying the warm April sunlight and noticing how green and crystal the grass looked and hearing the branches of the trees rustle and murmur in the light fresh wind. Everything was still, for the clinic-room behind me was quite deserted. They had not come to take me out to the ambulance yet.

Suddenly I heard a noise coming from the farther end of the gravel path. It was the sound of light footsteps. I looked up from the ground where I had been idly scattering some fallen leaves with my foot. I caught sight of something red moving through the trees at the top of the path. Then the figure rounded the little bend and came in view. It was a girl.

I bent my head again quickly and tried very hard to seem absorbed in kicking the trampled leaves hither and thither. I heard the footsteps come nearer. She must be very close to me now, I said to myself. I didn't want to look up, knowing that I might have to speak to her and knowing that I could not speak normally. "Don't be a fool," I said to myself.

I looked up timidly as the strange girl came to within a few feet of me. It was like seeing a vision. There was the green foliage of the trees in the background and the waving shadows of the branches on the dewy grass. The sun, from behind, was mingled with her fair hair, became diffused in it, so that it seemed as if a halo surrounded her. The radiance of the sun about her almost blinded me.

As she came forward, however, I saw she was a little above average height, brown haired and green eyed. Her features were of almost classical beauty; they seemed so clear cut, so finely chiseled and defined as to have been sculptured out of pure white marble. There was a fresh bloom on her cheeks that spring morning and a certain serenity in her eyes that made me stare and stare. It was rude of me, I knew, but I was quite helpless to look away. I remember telling myself quite distinctly as she advanced: "This is the most beautiful girl I've ever seen!"

Seeing no one about but me, she appeared to hesitate for a moment and then approached the chair firmly.

"Is Mr. Gallagher about, please?" she asked smiling.

I was absolutely tongue-tied. It wasn't only because of my usual speech difficulty.

In the end I spluttered out that Mr. Gallagher would be back soon, and she smiled again and went by me into the empty Clinic.

A week passed, and I was just about to give up hope of seeing her again when I came into the Clinic one Thursday morning and the first thing I saw as I was wheeled through the door was the same girl, kneeling on the floor beside one of the children, taking its coat off.

Slowly, bit by bit as the days went on, I got to know little things about her: she was a university graduate— that frightened me a little at first—she came from Galway, and, lastly, that her name was Sheila.

As I sat in my corner I watched her and saw how her hair tumbled about her face when she knelt and chatted with the children, how she brushed it back impatiently with a sweep of her arm. When she glanced across at me unexpectedly, I turned my head away in confusion and hummed a tune.

One morning, later, I was feeling particularly despondent within myself. I felt utterly miserable as I sat, leaning against the wall, my eyes downcast and my thoughts lost in a black pit of pessimism. I felt myself slipping back into the old mood of depression and hopelessness which now and then came sweeping back upon me out of the past. Then a voice said to me suddenly:

"Cheer up, Christy!"

I jerked around and found Sheila smiling at me encouragingly from the middle of the room. That one smile plucked the depression from me.

After that we began to know each other quite well. I began to go through my exercises with greater zest. Then, one morning, greatly daring, I brought her in a short story that I had begun to write. She took it home with her, read it, and returned it to me next morning with a little note inside containing her views of my future prospects as a "scribe."

Of course, I lost no time in replying to her note, and so we began corresponding with each other. Thus I had found one way of breaking down one of the greatest barriers, if not *the* greatest barrier, standing between me and other people—the great speech barrier. What I couldn't say with my lips I'd say through my pen.

The walls were indeed still very high around me, but I was scaling them one by one.

Scaling them—yes, breaking loose from them—yes. But what lay outside these walls? People spoke generally of freedom, of emancipation and release from physical affliction. But I found it wasn't just a question of overcoming, or at least fighting against my own handicap like a brave little hero and having them clap me on the back and tell me "I would get there soon." If by "there" they meant physical independence at last, that was all right, but if they also meant by it *complete* independence, complete freedom from all mental and emotional conflict, then they were quite wrong. Then all those fine-sounding words like "freedom" and "liberation" were hollow. For I was now finding out for myself that the pain and bitterness I had felt in the past during my "captivity," while I was still behind my prison bars, were as nothing compared with the pain and bitterness I now felt at the very time when I was struggling out of my chains, when my old hopelessness had been replaced by a fairly reasonable chance of recovery. I was now feeling the pain which clever people try to disguise under the name "awakening" or "enlightenment." This was no childish melancholy that came and went like April showers, but adult pain, which may have come and gone also, but which left a deeper impression, a deeper *scar* upon my mind. I felt myself coming to a greater, a more persistent awareness of my own needs, and that in itself was pain enough. But the pain went deeper when I also realized the impossibility of finding any adequate expression for such needs, when I saw that, no matter how I might overcome my physical limitations in time, my life, my inner, emotional life, the life that really mattered in the end, would never, *could* never really be normal. It would just have to lie bottled up inside me, suppressed instead of expressed.

In time, indeed, and with the help of the Clinic, I might so overcome myself—that I would be enabled to lead a normal life, or at least a more ordinary, more independent one. But I knew, deep inside me, that there would always be something missing—something that would never make the picture complete or let the pieces of the jigsaw fall finally into one perfect whole. There would always be a part of it missing. My affliction was not, after all, incurable. But something else was—my lack of really normal human expression and relationship. No matter how well I might conquer my handicap, I would never be a normal individual leading a normal life. The old difference would always remain. I wanted so desperately to love and be loved, but . . .

It was a bitter realization, but a true one, a necessary one. What good would it do me if I were to shut my eyes and turn my back on every unpleasant fact about myself? I was tempted to do that many times, but I was only putting off the final ordeal a little longer: it had to come some time. It came, it made me sad, bitter for a time, but in the end it also made me stronger within myself. If I could never really be like other people, then at least I would be like myself and make the best of it.

So it was that, ultimately, Sheila was the best friend that I could possibly have found. She was like a mirror in which I could see myself at last without disguise. She was the first milestone in my adult life, and through her I learned to travel the rest of the road without falling into any of the pitfalls along the way. We wrote a lot to one another, mine dreamy, fanciful letters, hers full of wisdom:

In one of your letters you say how some people think you a hero, and that you don't feel very heroic. I'm not very sure what a hero is, but here is my opinion of you: The good God gave you an excellent brain and an artistic streak. He also gave you a physical handicap. With the foregoing mental equipment your present struggle against your athetosis is inevitable. . . . Remember your mother, too, without whose good sense you might easily have turned into a most objectionable young man always talking of *what might have been* . . .

I have a little brown box at home in my study, closely guarded, inside which lies every one of the letters I got from Sheila, all bound together sentimentally with a piece of blue ribbon. Thirty-two in all. . . . I counted them the other day. . . .

13

THE PEN

MY EXPERIENCES AT the Clinic and the effect they had upon me made my mind full of ideas. It almost seemed as though a curtain had been lifted from before my eyes, as though I had at last found the key to something that had puzzled and tormented me for a long, long time.

I wanted desperately to say something, not merely to my family, not merely to my friends, but rather to everyone, to the world as a whole. There was something in me, some inner urge to speak, and I wanted to get it out of me, to communicate it to others and make them understand it. I felt I had found something, something I had been looking for ever since I began to think and feel about myself. It had taken years to find it, but now I was positive that I had discovered it at last, and suddenly I wanted to fling it to the four winds and let it go round the world, bearing its message into everyone's heart.

It wasn't just something about myself, but about all who had a life similar to my own, a life bounded and shut in on all sides by the high walls of a narrow, suppressed life. I felt that I had at last found a way of scaling those walls and breaking loose from the shadow of them, a way of taking my place in the sun and of playing my part in the world along with the able-bodied.

But—how could I express what I wanted to say, what I wanted everyone to know? My hands were of no use to me at all; they were still twisted and unruly, still powerless to grasp or hold anything. Nor could my lips utter the thoughts which were whirling round in my mind like swarms of impatient bees, because I still wasn't able to speak any sort of intelligible language outside the family circle, so that in general I was still tongue-tied, still doomed to a brooding silence.

What about my faithful old friend, my left foot? The foot that had served me so well and which had been my only weapon against despair and defeat through all those years? Could I not use that now?

No! That was impossible. I couldn't go back on my promise to Mrs. Collis. I'd think myself a traitor if I did. I had made a resolution and I was determined to keep to it.

Yet it wasn't just any irritating sense of loyalty that kept me from using my left foot. That in itself, I'm afraid, would not have been strong enough to help me resist the temptation. It was because I knew that if I started to use my foot again I would be standing in the way of my own recovery and making my chances of leading an active, if not a normal, life very much slimmer indeed. I had tied up my left foot and put it away, and I wasn't going to recall it to service now. It would be a sign of surrender anyway, and I wasn't prepared to wave the white flag yet.

It seemed I had reached a dead end; everywhere I turned the way was blocked. I felt the way anyone would feel with his hands and feet tied and a gag in his mouth.

Then, suddenly, I had an idea, an inspiration. I was sitting in the kitchen one afternoon thinking how I could find a way of putting down all I wanted to say on to paper when I noticed one of my brothers sitting over a copy-book at the table with a pen in his hand, writing something into it. This was Eamonn, just twelve years of age at the time, and he was doing his homework—an English composition, which I could see, by the scowl on his face, he wasn't enjoying very much. The idea of him sitting there writing and yet not knowing what to write about, and me sitting there by the window, my brain teeming with ideas and yet not able to hold a pen in my hand, almost made me want to jump up from the chair and run amok!

Instead, I leaned forward and asked him what he was doing.

"Trying to write a composition for school," answered Eamonn with a sigh. "I'll get biffed if I don't do it right."

I saw my chance. I told him I'd help him—on condition that he'd do something for me in return.

"Sure I will," he said confidently. "What do you want me to do?"

"Write for me," I told him briefly.

His face fell. "But I can't even do my own writing!" he protested, "I wouldn't know what to say!"

"Fool," I replied. "You'll just hold the pen and I'll tell you what to put down."

My brother was very doubtful about this idea; it sounded too complicated to him and he felt sure there was something fishy at the back of it. But at the same time he wanted to get that composition right, so in the end he agreed to my condition and I did his homework for him.

When we were done, we went out to my study at the back of the house, got a nine-penny jotter out of the drawer, sat down at the table and looked at each other.

"What d'ye want me to write down for you?" asked my brother innocently, the pen poised in his hand.

I looked out the window at the branches of the trees waving against the bright spring sky, thought a bit, then turned back to look at my young brother's inquiring face.

"My life story," I told him.

Poor Eamonn let his pen clatter down on the table.

"Your . . . what?" he asked.

I told him again, and this time he was quite silent.

In the end I got him to agree to write for me for "an indefinite period." We started that very afternoon, without any sort of preparation whatever.

I was eighteen when I began that first attempt to write my autobiography. It was a ponderous piece of work, a veritable forest of seven- and eight-syllabled words. My only reading up to this had been Dickens, and in my inexperience I imagined it my duty to try and imitate his style of writing—with the result that the English I used was fifty years out of date! I used words and phrases that would have tied up anybody's tongue in a matter of seconds. So long were the words that I had to spell them letter by letter, before my brother could write them down on the page. I am still wondering why neither of us had a nervous breakdown during the writing of that tremendous first attempt. It must have amounted to tens of thousands of words before I became discouraged. It dragged on and on sluggishly, like a stream of molten lead. My poor brother often got writer's cramp. He had written almost four hundred pages of manuscript before I saw that if I went on like this the book would go on forever.

Its title typified the whole. I called it "The Reminiscences of a Mental Defective." I meant that to be a nice piece of irony, a sort of punch on the nose for the doctors who had doubted my sanity at the age of five.

The language, if impossible, was gorgeous. For instance, instead of calling myself a cripple and leaving it at that, I spoke of myself as being an "unfortunate item of mortality," and again as a "heavenly miscarriage." I was also very fond of changing a straightforward word into an obscure one by putting "ism" at the end of it: instead of saying "defeat" I said "defeatism," and I was also adept at using completely abstract words to express my essentially simple ideas: words like "inconceivability" when I wanted to describe a thing that couldn't happen, "incongruous" for something that didn't fit, and I used the word "materialistic" very often when what I really had in mind was something thoughtless and gay, so that, in my twisted conception of things at that time, I could have said my brother Peter was a materialist because he preferred going to dances and parties to reading Dickens!

The other day I pulled out part of this famous manuscript.

In the first chapter I gave a description of my home life: ". . . I was brought up amid an environment of working-class doctrination and morality. As the world knows, the pursuit of literary . . . knowledge is not widely practised by this class of the human race. . . . Intellectualism is not a characteristic of this breed. . . ."

Anyone's guess is as good as mine as to the meaning of that last sentence!

On page thirty-two I was still on the subject of the working class: "While admitting that class and social differentiation is necessary for the harmonious development of mankind, I also consider that such segregation should be confined within the realms of moderation, thus preventing unnecessary prejudice and superfluous social friction. . . ."

And that was well before I even had an idea of what the word "social" meant!

All this, of course, didn't mean that I didn't know what I wanted to say, but the trouble was that I didn't know *how* to say it. I hadn't as yet found a way of expressing my thoughts clearly and putting them into intelligible form. Indeed then, I seemed to be quite determined never to make a simple statement if I could turn it into a complex one. I seldom expressed one individual thought in a single sentence. I required three or four sentences before being satisfied that I'd really expressed my meaning, and sometimes I would use up a whole paragraph to express a single thought. I could never resist digressing—or, as my father would say, "beating about the bush."

The passage that I now quote shows how clearly the effect Dickens had on me, because it is so typically Dickensian that it might almost have come from between the covers of any one of his books.

". . . It is when we are released from the turbulence and feverish activity of day that we fall, without conscious effort or mental volition, into a reverie mingled with regrets and mellow joys. . . . All the happy and tearful scenes of the forgotten past crowd before our inner eye. . . . We re-live again the trials and pleasures we have been through . . . we recall all our little vanities and pretences. . . . We exclaim to ourselves: 'This wasn't me! I was never as reckless as that, surely!' . . . Yet the past never lies: it is irrevocable . . . would that it were not so! What an abundance of saints and angels there would be then! . . ."

I was eighteen when I perpetrated that!

The pages of manuscript just kept piling up, stack upon stack. I went on dictating and my brother went on taking it down till we both reached the stage when I spoke and he wrote mechanically, without exactly knowing what we were doing. We were just going round in circles. I still had a vague idea that I was supposed to be writing my life story, but I didn't seem to be getting anywhere. I kept talking and Eamonn kept writing and the copybooks kept filling up day by day. It was just a forest of words, with no clear path through it.

I knew there was something wrong somewhere, for before I'd begin dictating, my thoughts would be clear enough, but the moment I began trying to dictate them, they'd all go haywire, they'd all become twisted and go scattering around in my mind like fallen leaves blown to and fro by the wind. I found it hard to catch and hold on to them. I became mad at my own stupidity.

I called myself a fool, I called my poor brother a fool. In fact, I called everyone in the house a fool—because I couldn't write as well as I wanted to! The longer the book dragged on, the more irritable I became. If anything got in my way, I'd just lift my foot and kick it violently. I'd get so annoyed that sometimes I wanted to burn the whole thing and put it out of my sight, but I hadn't the heart to do away with it. I had by this time spent nearly two years at it and I couldn't bear to admit, even to myself, that all that work had been in vain, that I had failed. I was too stubborn to give in and throw it all into the fire. I knew, I felt that I could write a good book, if only—if only. . . .

That was it! If only I had someone to advise me, to show me how to write clearly and constructively with no gaps between or holes in the middle! Someone who would know what he was talking about, who would put me on to the right path. I needed a guiding hand; I needed someone not only with brains but with a heart as well.

But where could I find this somebody, this fairy godfather? Not in Kimmage, anyway! This was a house of bricklayers only: my brothers knew nothing about writing, and I knew nothing about laying bricks, so that was that.

I thought and thought, but I could think of no one. It looked as though I was entirely on my own. It seemed as if I'd have to carry on by myself as best I could, torturously trying to express myself and only getting more and more lost as I went on.

Then one day, as I was sitting moodily by the window in a bad temper, too disgusted with myself even to dictate any more, a name suddenly flashed across my mind, so suddenly that I almost fell off the chair: "Collis!" I heard myself saying out loud, "Collis!" Without waiting to think, I yelled for Eamonn, made him get a postcard from the drawer and sent it to Dr. Collis immediately. I was very abrupt—I just wrote this little message:

"Dear Dr. Collis. I'm trying to write a book. If you don't mind, please come and help me. Christy Brown."

It was only after the card had been posted that I began to think about what I had done. I hadn't seen the doctor for over a year, not since I had come back from London. I didn't know much about him, except that he was the founder of the Clinic and chief of the Cerebral Palsy Association of Ireland. I had liked him from the moment I saw him. I hadn't felt any embarrassment or awkwardness in his presence the first time I met him, and that was unusual, because even with people I knew quite well I always felt out of place. Sometimes I felt the same way even with my family.

But, after all, he was only a doctor, wasn't he? He might be the nicest man in the world, but what good was that if he couldn't help me to write? Apart from being a nice man, who was he?

It was only later that I found out that he was not just Dr. Collis—but Robert Collis, the author, too, the man who had written the famous play, *Marrowbone Lane, The Silver Fleece,* his own autobiography, along with other plays and books.

The next day I was in my little study at the rear of the house, sitting by the fire reading old Dickens, when the door opened suddenly and Dr. Collis marched in, carrying a large bundle of books under one arm and a briefcase in the other. He dumped the books on the bed, put the case on the floor, and turned round.

"Hello," he said, coming over and sitting down on the chair at the opposite side of the table. "I got your S.O.S. this morning. So you're writing a book. Well, let's see it."

I had the manuscript stored away in an old leather case under the bed. He got down on his knees, pulled it out, took out the manuscript, brought it over to the table, put on his glasses, and began reading.

As he read the first page I saw him raise his eyebrows. He read the second and the third, and each time his eyebrows went higher. Then he threw down the copy on the table and looked up at me.

"What the hell!" he said and stopped.

He looked at me keenly to see if I could take criticism and understand. I forced myself to keep a poker face. He smiled.

"Yes, it's awful—" he said, "the language you use may have been popular in the reign of Queen Victoria, but . . ."

My heart sank within me as I heard this. It looked hopeless. It seemed that I would never do what I now wanted to do more than anything else—write my life story. It seemed I was back to where I always had been, wanting to do things and not knowing how. My dreams were too big to come true. How could I ever write a book—I, who had been shut up all my life behind the four walls of my home and who had never so much as seen the inside of a schoolroom? I was mad even to think of such an idea.

This passed through my mind as Robert Collis sat before me, turning over the pages of that awful manuscript.

Sometimes he grunted to himself. I sat with my head bowed.

Suddenly he stopped and sat upright in the chair. I looked up in surprise. His face was smiling with approval.

"Good!" he exclaimed excitedly, slapping the table with his hand. "You have written one sentence here that stands out like a rose among a lot of weeds, one shining little gem thrown in among stones. It shows me that you could write literature if you knew how. That's what I wanted to find out."

Then he got up and had a look at the few books I had on the shelves. He shook his head.

"To write good modern English one has to read modern English, Christy. Dickens is all very well, but . . . literary taste, like all other tastes, changes."

Then he showed me the books he had brought me, and spread them all out on the table. There was a book of L.A.G. Strong's short stories, two books by Seàn O'Faolain, some books of his literary brothers, John Stewart and Maurice Collis, and six volumes of a collection of famous literature from all over the world.

"These will show you how good English should be written," he said.

He told me that if I wanted to be a writer I must learn to write. That writing was as difficult an art as painting, and to master it one had to practice it and cultivate a style of one's own bit by bit. He told me that, no matter how difficult I found it, I had one good thing in my favor—I *wanted* to write, I had the inclination, and that was as important as having a style, which I could develop as I went on. To do a thing really well, one had to like doing it. A good style was pretty useless if there was nothing behind it. Writing like that was like a taste without the food.

He then sat down and took up the manuscript, looking at it again thoughtfully. He was silent for some time. I could hear the fire crackling, the clock ticking loudly on the mantelshelf, and the faint sound of voices coming from the kitchen across the yard. At last he spoke.

"Christy," he said, leaning forward with his elbows rest-

ing on the table, "all this—" pointing to the bundle of
copies—"hasn't been in vain. It may be unreadable, but
it hasn't been a waste. If it has done nothing else, it has
given you lots of practice at thinking out ideas. If you still
want to write your story—?" He paused and looked at me
questioningly. I nodded my head vigorously: I wanted to
write that story above everything else.

"Right, then," he went on, getting up from the table
and pacing the room. "If so, you must begin the whole
thing again!" Now he began to talk, to teach me. I realized
later that he was a teacher and had many students. "There
are two first principles attached to writing any sort of
story," he said, "first, you must *have* a story to tell, and
secondly, you must tell it in such a way that the person
reading it can live in it himself. Now let me give you some
concrete points: Whenever you can, use a short word
rather than a long one. You have painted pictures with a
brush, try and do the same thing with a pen. Practice it.
Just describe the room here: your queer chair, the picture
on the smudged wall there, the broken mirror, the books,
that colored photograph. . . ."

I listened, as I had never listened before, that evening
and many following while he taught me how to write. I
never forgot one thing he said.

At last he came over to me and shook hands. I knew
then that I was about to start on the toughest job I had
ever taken on, but with this man behind me, I knew that I
would see it done one day. . . . I knew it in his hand-
shake.

14

PRIDE, NOT PITY

THE MERRION STREET CLINIC, as I have said, was really only a long, narrow gymnasium hut at the rear of the Dublin Orthopaedic Hospital which couldn't be reached very easily. Apart from its out-of-the-way position, the space it afforded was very cramped indeed. Everything was on top of everything else—the children included. There wasn't much room for equipment, except for a large wooden "slide" which was pushed close against one wall and which took up nearly one side of the room. This contraption was not merely for the amusement of the children: it served another purpose as well. It had a small flight of stairs attached to it with a sort of platform at the top. This gave some of the children much good practice at climbing steps and using their hands in holding on to the rails as they went up, thus being taught to use both hands and feet at the same time, an action which many of them couldn't do under normal circumstances, except in a very jerky, irregular way. As they slid down the long chute they slowly learned to relax and overcome their fear of movement.

The Clinic, however, was becoming overcrowded.

"If this keeps up," said Dr. Warnants one day, "we'll have to start putting them on the roof."

It looked like that, for the room often resembled a traffic jam, and the children yelled louder than a dozen car horns honking all together. It was so bad that sometimes I could hardly hear myself think!

Things were getting desperate when I suddenly heard that we were going to move to another part of the city to bigger premises situated on a more convenient site. I was sorry to leave the old Clinic, even though I knew it was much too small. I felt sentimental about it, for I had made many good friends there. I remembered the first morning I came to it: the brown wooden walls, the high windows, the trees outside dripping with December rain, and Sheila. . . .

It was about this time that we lost Dr. Warnants, who left to take up a post abroad. We were all sorry to see him go, but somehow I always felt that he had the wanderlust in him, the urge to travel to faraway places. The last time I heard from him he was in the Far East, "sweltering in the midday sun," as he put it.

Mr. Gallagher, too, left soon afterwards for Canada. He vanished. I never heard anything of him after that. So it seemed that just as the Clinic was about to be improved, two of its ablest workers left.

It was on a warm summer morning three years ago that we came to the new Clinic for the first time. It was in a place called Bull Alley Street. Looking at it from the street outside, I saw it was a big, red-bricked building, very tall, with handsome arches and a sort of green cupola on the top. It had many large windows in front and wrought-iron railings all around. Compared to the old Clinic, it was a very "posh" place indeed.

It was even better inside. We didn't own the whole building—in fact, we only had a loan of three rooms from the trustees. But the rooms were large and sunny, and everyone had plenty of space to move around in. Everything was much better organized; the staff became bigger, the attendance became bigger, and the standard of treatment and progress much better. The rooms were divided into three—the treatment-room, the schoolroom and the playroom. In the treatment-room, of course, we receive our exercises, which are often quite a spectacle as fifteen and sometimes twenty children lie on the floor and follow the instructions of the physiotherapists, the kids looking, as they lie in a row on the ground, like a huge serpent with many heads, arms, and legs, all moving in unison.

In the schoolroom, the more backward of the children, those who have never been able to attend normal schools with their sisters and brothers because of their difference, are given an ordinary primary education under a qualified National teacher who is specially trained for such a difficult task. Thus, one more gulf is bridged, one more link is forged in helping those children to establish ordinary contact with ordinary people. They are very proud of the fact that they, too, can "go to school" and have books and desks and learn sums like their sisters and brothers at home. They are always boasting about *their* teacher and the way she helps them. *They* never get "biffed" like the children in the "common" schools. In their school their teacher concentrates more upon their minds than upon their hands. In this way, instead of feeling inferior to normal children, they are taught to think of themselves as equals.

In the playroom a lot goes on. Here the word "play" has a double meaning: it also means work. Under the guise of playing, the children are taught to develop proper hand and foot movements and to displace wrong ones. To a stranger who might be looking on, they seem to be just playing at the tables and running about the same as ordinary children, all the time making an awful lot of noise. That is so. They *are* encouraged to go about and behave like ordinary children with this difference, that while they run so happily about, they are constantly being watched to see that they do not relapse into their original wrong physical movements. It is not enough to run about—they must be taught to run about *properly,* to play and chase around the room *in the right way.* They were denied the use of natural movements, and so developed wrong unnatural ones instead. In the playroom they learn to make every movement, from the smallest to the biggest, as natural and free as possible. Nothing comes "easy" to them. Even the simple act of picking up a piece of chalk from the floor is a tremendous task to some of the children, as big a task as walking on a tightrope would be to someone who had never learned that technique.

Since I have been coming to the Clinic almost from its birth, I have come to regard it as being in some way a part of me, a necessary part of my life. I don't just think of it as a place where I come to get treatment for my affliction, as a medical institution filled with doctors and white-coated physiotherapists. It has its doctors and its persons in white, it has its long corridors and cool marble walls: it has all these, but it has something else besides. It has *spirit* as well as efficiency, genuine human warmth as well as cold scientific precision. The people in the cool white coats have very warm hearts, and in their job a warm heart is an invaluable asset. It counts just as much as their medical skill, for theirs is not an ordinary straightforward job because theirs are not ordinary patients. They are not just medical people treating patients. They are a set of human beings deeply and sincerely interested in the plight of another set of human beings faced with many huge problems, problems which cannot merely be summarized under the heading "physical."

We need confidence and friendliness as well as, if not more than, medical treatment. It is not only our muscles and limbs which bother us—sometimes it is our minds as well, our inner selves that require more attention than our twisted arms and legs. A child with a crooked mouth and twisted hands can very quickly and easily develop a set of very crooked and twisted attitudes both towards himself and life in general, especially if he is allowed to grow up with them without being helped to an understanding of them. If the idea of his difference as compared to normal children is allowed to take root in his mind, it will grow with him into adolescence and eventually into manhood, so that he will look out on life with a mind as distorted as his body might be. Life becomes for him just a reflection of his own "crookedness," his own emotional pain.

In the Clinic, it is different. Here, we are among our own, so to speak. We are surrounded by people with handicaps similar to, and often worse than, our own, and we see that our old difference is not so different after all. From thinking of ourselves as outcasts and burdens on others, we slowly come to realize that there are people who understand, people who have actually dedicated their lives towards helping us and bringing us to a greater understanding of our own, so that in the end something splendid is wrought out of our affliction.

Bernie, one of the children attending the Clinic, is a great favorite of mine, as she is with everyone. She is an excellent example of what the Clinic can do for even "hopeless" cases.

She was one of the first patients at the Clinic. She was only two years old when I first saw her. We came along to the Clinic in the same ambulance every morning, and I remember what a pathetic little scrap she was then. I used to watch her as she lay before me on the stretcher, but all I could see of her were her eyes, staring out of a tiny elfin face. She was so small and diminutive that her eyes seemed to be the biggest part of her. She lay completely inert, like something that had neither warmth nor life, just a stiff, huddled-up thing that seemed cold and insensible to all around—except for the eyes, which alone showed that this was a human creature, this thing wrapped up in the blanket like a child's doll.

Slowly, bit by bit, she began to display more life and to take more interest in the things that were going on about her, as though she were gradually thawing out.

The stage was reached when she could be given exercises specially worked out for her, and today Bernie is one of the Clinic's liveliest patients as well as being one of its showpieces. Under the careful tuition of Miss Dorothy Henderson, the physiotherapist who looks after her, Bernie has evolved from being an inert bundle of clothes, motionless as a block of wood, into a vivacious, pretty little creature, now beginning to chatter and giggle. Miss Henderson describes he as "a coaxing wench."

Her greatest rival at the Clinic is Dorothy, and to watch them together, each trying to outdo the other at exercises, is much better than a pantomime.

Dorothy is a very important little person and very charming too. She was one of the worst cases to arrive at the Clinic, but she has improved so much since then that many people who saw her at the start of her treatment can hardly recognize her as the same little girl today. To begin with, she could barely manage to sit up at all.

Her back sagged, her shoulders drooped, and her head lolled from side to side like a daisy tossed by the wind. She would try to crawl from place to place, but her hands and knees failed to support her and she'd just double up and fall flat on her face.

By degrees, as the months went on, she was taught, first of all, to relax on a blanket spread out on the floor, then to improve her sitting posture, and, finally, to stand a little with the barest minimum of support.

Next thing that had to be tackled was her walking, and for this she had to wear specially made wooden "skis" to give her good hand support, proper foot position, and to improve her stance generally.

Now Dorothy is able to move about *properly* on her hands and knees and is beginning to take a few slow, hesitant steps on her own. She is one of the most charming little creatures imaginable, with her large, limpid brown eyes, her scattered black curls and the little snub nose that always wrinkles up when she smiles that coy, infectious smile of hers.

Dorothy is also a potential physiotherapist. She has a very agile mind that takes everything in, and during her years at the Clinic she has seen enough of physiotherapy to be quite eager to show off to the staff what she can do in that line herself. There is nothing she likes better than to crawl over to where one of the smaller children lies, squat down beside it, and proceed to give it "its exercises" in no uncertain fashion, including an odd slap or two if the poor kid's performance doesn't meet with her ladyship's approval.

Sometimes, Dorothy becomes overambitious, toddles across the room and tries to experiment on me as well. But I always exasperate her by remaining impassive and just grinning at her when she orders me to bend my leg, pull in my tummy and keep my seat down.

I myself have improved quite a lot within the last two years at the Clinic. The first job I had to be taught was to relax. That may sound easy, but I find it the most difficult part of the morning's work. To relax isn't just a question of lying down on the bed or floor and remaining like a log; it isn't as simple as that. Complete relaxation is something that even very few normal people can claim to possess. To relax one's muscles completely, to make them as limp as wet paper, it is necessary to relax one's mind first, to give one's thoughts free rein and let them wander where they will without any conscious guidance or inclination toward any particular object. That is something I find nearly impossible. I have a very restless mind. The only time it relaxes is when I am asleep, and I am not a very good sleeper! Even when I have succeeded in getting my arms and legs still, it isn't always a sign that I am relaxed —I may only be *keeping* them still by keeping them tense. It is easy to *look* relaxed, but not so easy to *feel* relaxed. Trying to force yourself to relax is one of the worst things you can do, because in that way you only pile up your bodily tension and get further and further away from real relaxation. I am always intensely aware of the scene around me: the noise, the interplay and interchange of light and shade, the particular expressions on the faces of the people around me, the tones and inflections of voices. They all register themselves on my mind clearly and distinctly, like pebbles dropped in a lake.

Not until I can really relax properly will I be able to convince myself that I have accomplished anything that others like me couldn't do with the same guidance. Today, working under the expert instructions of Dr. Mary O'Donnell, who now supervises the Clinic, and Miss Barbara Allen, one of the three physiotherapists who form the staff, I have reached the stage where I am now learning to walk in specially made skis, like those which little Dorothy uses, except on a much bigger scale, and to make more use of my hands.

The Clinic's oldest member, its "mater," is Mrs. Frances Prince. She joined it in the days when its future was still very uncertain, and she has been with us ever since. With her about I can do no dodging or shirking, as I sometimes feel like on a bad morning. She never fails to find lots of work for me when I'm sitting at the table such as molding shapes out of sticks of plasticine—they usually turn out to be the most unshapely shapes imaginable!—manipulating dumbbells from one hand to the other, all good hand exercises for me, and so on.

Speech has always been one of the biggest obstacles in my endeavor to make ordinary contact with people. It has been the one aspect of my handicap that has caused me the bitterest pain, for without speech one is practically lost, curtained off from other people, left wishing to say a million things and not able to say one. Writing is all very well, but there are some emotions that cannot be conveyed, that cannot be "felt" through the written word alone. Writing may be immortal, but it does not bridge the gap between two human beings as the voice may, and oh, I would rather have an hour's fierce argument with a pal or a few moments of soft chatter with a girl than write the greatest book on earth.

Now, however, I am beginning to speak more and grunt less. My old grunt is becoming a little more dignified, a little more articulate. This is due to the special treatment I have been receiving from the Clinic's speech therapist, Dr. Patricia Sheehan.

I must admit I was a little disconcerted when I first began this treatment. It had such a big name, "speech therapy," and yet its methods were so simple that I felt anyone could have thought them out. It looked mere child's play.

How mistaken I was! The methods *were* simple—that was the point of them, but their results were tremendous. The first lesson I learned was to breathe properly and deeply. She told me that I had got into the habit of breathing anyhow, in jerks. That wouldn't do, she said. I would never speak properly unless I learned how to control my breathing.

She took me in hand straight away. The first breathing lesson I had was—blowing bubbles! One morning she brought in a little tin box filled with soapy water, took out from her pocket a tiny metal ring with a handle on it, dipped it into the water, and then told me to blow away the watery film that had formed inside the ring. I looked at her, thinking it was a joke. But I saw she was serious, so I took a breath, pursed up my lips, and blew. Immediately a perfect hail of brightly colored bubbles began falling about me from all angles. One burst on my nose, another in my eye, and I could see that her hair was spangled with dozens of vapory balls! I started to hum "I'm Forever Blowing Bubbles."

Then very soon it became a little tougher. Along with my friend John, another adult patient attending the Clinic, I was taught to increase and deepen my breathing in rather a novel way. This consisted in blowing water through a tube from one bottle to another. The two bottles were airtight, and a rubber tube ran from one into the other and both ends of this were connected to two tiny glass cylinders inserted in the corks. One of the bottles would be filled with colored water, and the plan was to blow the contents of the full bottle through the connecting tube into the empty one and gradually fill it.

It sounds simple, but I found it very hard indeed. Like the big bad wolf in the old fairy tale, I puffed and I puffed till I was red in the face, but only a miserable few drops of water trickled through into the empty bottle. John's turn came next and in a matter of seconds he had blown all the water from one bottle into the other, for John has a first-class pair of lungs. I was very disappointed with myself, but as time went on I became a little better at the water-blowing business, though so far I am still not a patch on him.

I found after some months that my speech had improved considerably: I took greater care to make certain I articulated each word slowly and distinctly and to say what I wanted to say calmly and without any of my usual fuss. Now I can speak quite well if only I take my time about it and do not get flustered when I cannot get out a word clearly. Basically, the whole cause of my speech difficulty lies in my own attitude to it. Once I have conquered that queer hot feeling of panic, almost of shame, that brings the blood in a warm swift rush to my cheeks whenever anyone strange tries to converse with me, I will have destroyed the root cause of my trouble.

Today I am speaking with greater self-confidence and less self-consciousness. I know that I can never lead a full, healthy social life unless I can speak so that others will understand me, and to achieve that end I must work hard and practice long. It will not be easy and I can never expect perfection or a job on the B.B.C., but the great progress I have made under Dr. Sheehan is an indication that if I try hard enough it's not impossible—and I shall certainly try.

The staff has great patience with me, for I am not in any way a model patient. Miss Henderson says I am very much inclined to be lazy and that I don't put enough earnestness into my work at the Clinic. I should like to contradict her, but I'm afraid I can't because what she says is true. I know that, in many ways, I don't try hard enough, or at least not as hard as I may have made people think by all I have just said. It is not, however, because I don't give my treatment the seriousness and importance it deserves, for I know that my daily few hours at the Clinic every morning are the most important part of my whole day. I may be lazy, too, in some ways. But perhaps if anyone looked deep enough they might find that the old pen had a lot to do with it too. . . .

The children at the Clinic are happy children, from the little ones who wriggle about on the floor and kick their heels in the air to the bigger ones who chase and play around the room and tumble over one another now and then. They are brought to and from the Clinic by people who voluntarily drive them in their own private cars two or three days, sometimes every morning of the week, from Monday to Friday. The children look forward to the drive from their homes to the Clinic and the attachment that grows between children and driver is often a deep and very touching one. The moment the driver comes to take them home again at noon those children that are able come crowding round her—or him—and chatter away excitedly about the morning's work, while those that can't move just yell and kick their legs happily as they lie on the floor. Every one of the children loves coming to the Clinic, because they not only receive treatment—which by itself just wouldn't be enough—but they also receive the kind of sympathy and understanding which they need more than anything else, an understanding that goes deeper than just mere kind words, and a sympathy that is without pity.

The women who form the staff—Dr. Mary O'Donnell, Dr. Patricia Sheehan, Mrs. Frances Prince, Miss Dorothy Henderson, Miss Barbara Allen, Miss Joyce McCrory and Miss Una Kennedy, the schoolteacher—have all done, and are doing, a splendid job, and their skill and resourcefulness need no limelight from me. They all emanate friendliness and understanding, and though it is necessary for them to be a little stern now and then when their charges become lazy and inattentive, that sternness never hardens into coldness, for no matter how strict they may become, one can see a light, a glow on their faces and in their eyes as they look over the heads of the children at one another, for to enter the Clinic is to enter at once into its spirit, the spirit that animates and flows through it like a wave, surging forth from eye to eye and heart to heart, and it is the spirit of *pride not pity*.

15

CLICHÉS AND CAESAR

I WENT ON learning more and more about writing from Robert Collis as time went on. He taught me so many things in so short a time that for a few days I was rather dizzy, like one who suddenly comes upon a treasure chest of jewels and is blinded by their light. He would come into my little study, sit down, and start talking to me about writing in a simple way without using any grand phrases or introducing any vague theories. He had something to tell me, something he wanted me to know, and he lost no time in teaching me it as plainly and as clearly as he could.

It was still very difficult for us to discuss things together properly, for so far I still couldn't speak to anyone outside the family without becoming awkward and embarrassed and feeling my face grow red. I was still very shut up in myself in spite of everything. So he did all the talking, and I did all the listening.

Slowly I began to get some idea of the vast world of literature—its forms and standards, its principles and conventions, its subtleties and uniqueness, but, above all, its calm, its beauty and fascination. I saw it as a temple of human thought and ideals, built up of many kinds of minds, from the humble to the great, from the mere recorder and historian to the great thinker, from men who wrote with their minds only to those who wrote with their hearts, their very souls as well.

In the light of all that I learned from him, I saw the many mistakes I had made. But he was very patient. He came out to me whenever he could make it, sometimes twice and even three times a week. He taught me the technicalities without being technical: he was a good critic and did not let my situation soften his criticism. But he believed in me, believed I could become a writer, and that gave me the confidence I needed.

Soon I started to write the second version of my autobiography, still by dictation. My scribe now was Francis, my thirteen-year-old brother, a short-trousered schoolboy, quite different from Eamonn and Seàn, who just wrote down what I said, without thinking, like a pair of writing machines. He thought about what he was writing. After we had finished for the day, or night as was often the case, he would sit down quietly and read over what he had written down for me, sometimes asking me many questions about the grammar, the construction, the meaning of words, and so on, questions which I was hard put to answer at times. One night I asked him what he thought of a chapter which we had just finished. He thought for a while, twiddling the pen between his fingers, then looked up and said very solemnly:

"It's all right, but you'd want the dictionary beside you when reading it!"

I wanted to throw the table at him, but he just sat there, not a smile on his face, his hands folded placidly in his lap. I was furious, but I knew there was something in what he said.

The second effort at writing the book came out much better than the first. The theme was more clear cut, the construction more orderly and correlated, and the thought behind it more mature. I hoped for a while that it might do, but still Dr. Collis shook his head.

"Better than before," he said. "But not good enough yet. You're still too literary."

It was true. I was still inclined to be pompous and unnecessarily dramatic. A lot of what I said rang false, and I was still very fond of rambling off and talking about things that had nothing to do with the book.

"Scrap it and start over again," he said. "This time you can make it, I know. We've all written and rewritten our stuff, often desperately, till we got it right—third time lucky."

I pretended to smile, but actually I swore to myself as I contemplated the awful piles of useless manuscript. Would it never come out right?

"Another thing, Christy," he said one night. "You use too many clichés. Do you know what a cliché is?"

I didn't: it sounded like some kind of foreign animal or insect. But I found out that it was "something that everybody said," a figure of speech that was in common usage, words and phrases which were used so often both in books and ordinary conversation that they had become thin and shiny, things that have been said over and over again until they become hackneyed and their original meaning lost.

When I found out this, I knew that I was frightfully guilty of this sin. Only yesterday I sat beside "the roaring fire"; I heard "the screeching wind"; I waited "in an agony of suspense"; I saw she had "lustrous eyes, full, inviting lips and a swanlike neck, and hair like floating strands of gossamer"; I "had a lump in my throat"; and someone was "swearing like a trooper!"

I found on looking back over my manuscript that I had

used so many clichés, so many times, that the number must have run into hundreds.

I found also that I seemed exceptionally partial to purple patches, which bobbed up here and there like corks in a tub of water. Like the clichés, they were almost unsuppressible. I was still very much like the old mockingbird, very fond of imitating others.

One December night, two years ago, Dr. Collis came into my study and sat down on the seat opposite me. He said nothing for a while, but just sat, warming his hands at the fire. Then he pushed his chair away a bit and looked up.

"Christy," he said, "I've been thinking about your future. You have talent for original work. The problem is how best to develop it. How far have you got in your education?"

My education! It was practically nil. The first and only bit of education I ever had was learning the alphabet from mother at the age of five. I had gone on from there the best way I could on my own, teaching myself to read books—mostly Dickens!—and to learn all I could from them. Education! The very word made me tremble in the middle, for I knew, or rather felt, that all I had taught myself through childhood and adolescence was nothing, and I knew that I had a long way to go before I started to know what knowledge is.

"Not very far," I managed to say.

"I see," he said. "Education is invaluable, and in your case I think it is essential."

He lapsed into silence again, his foot tapping on the tiled hearthstone and one hand pulling at a button on his waistcoat. I waited.

"You couldn't attend a school or university in the ordinary way," he went on, "so the next best thing is to get a private tutor for you. Someone with a sound knowledge of human nature who would be intelligent enough to disregard your unusual physical movements and lack of speech. I'm going to ask the Marrowbone Lane Fund to put up the money."

A few days later he came and told me that, with the help of Katriona Maguire he had found the ideal sort of man to school me, a master in one of the large National schools in Kimmage who lived quite close to my own home.

"I think you'll get on well together," he said. "He's the sort of tutor any boy would wish to have."

The very next evening a priest of the parish, Father Mullane, came along with my new tutor and introduced me to him. I was sitting by the window, reading a book by Jacques Maritain when the door opened and the priest and the strange man entered, led by mother.

"This is Mr. Guthrie, Christy," said Father Mullane.

I looked up and saw before me a short, stocky, fresh-complexioned man, of about middle age, with keen blue eyes and a humorous mouth. I noticed how deliberate and precise were all his movements and little gestures, and how expressive were his arched eyebrows. His whole face seemed lit with a keen intelligence and a keener sympathy. I felt the force and attraction of his personality in that first moment of meeting him and I took an instant liking to him.

"Hello, Christy," he said in a deep resonant voice, coming forward and shaking hands with me. "I'm delighted to meet you. I hope we'll be partners from now on."

And that was the way of it. Mr. Guthrie began at once to show his skill by breaking down quietly, steadily, and very confidently all the barriers that naturally stood in the way. The relationship that grew between us was friendly, practical, and unassuming. He made me feel as if we were partners in a big and difficult job. He led me forward.

He came twice a week, usually on Monday and Wednesday evenings, each session lasting for about two hours or more. For the first month or so I felt very backward and ill at ease in his presence, and I was painfully conscious of the defect in my speech when answering his questions. But after a time the first bit of awkwardness wore off and we both became accustomed to each other and settled down to the job in hand. Indeed, so settled did I become that I began speaking quite freely, becoming at times very loquacious. When the official program was over for the night, he would stay on for a while and we'd discuss many things, like the philosophy of Bertrand Russell, the poetry of Thompson and Yeats, or what psychoanalysis was, so that, apart from the ordinary lessons, I learned a great deal. And, of course, those talks greatly helped me to speak clearly and confidently.

When I was first introduced to mathematics, I couldn't write down the figures myself, so I had to recall Seàn to service, as Francis had more than enough work to do on the next version of the book. Besides, Seàn was pretty good at math in school and he proved to be a help to me in both arithmetic and algebra—almost too good a help, in fact, for pretty soon I found myself letting him do all the dirty work, tackling the hard core of the stuff while I just corrected the answers. I tried to discover some interest or pleasure in equations, compound interest, rates and precentages, and all the rest, but they only made me sick and my head ache. In spite of this, however, I came on bit by bit, though I always hated figures.

Funny though, when I came to geometry I actually liked it. I almost reveled in solving theorems and problems on angles, triangles, parallelograms, areas, rectangles and so on. I don't know why I liked this branch of mathematics and hated the rest. But the fact is, I liked it immensely and was very content spending hours at it.

Then came Latin, which I took to at once. I fell in love with the elegance and beauty of the language, its smoothness and neatness of expression and its delicate shades and tones of meaning. After the first year of softening up, I was introduced to Caesar through the medium of his *Gallic War,* which I found rather heavy, but still quite interesting.

My reading also became more up to date and comprehensive. Before Sheila had left for America to be married two years before she gave me a large and very beautiful volume of the complete works of Shakespeare, which is now my dearest possession. I remember how, on the morning she left the Clinic for good, she got me to recite for her Hamlet's heartbreaking speech, "To be or not to be." As I spoke it, all the children were shouting and laughing around us. She sat before me, the engagement ring sparkling on her finger in a shaft of sunlight.

Discovering all the beauty of Shakespeare gave me an almost physical sense of joy. Often while in the middle of one of his plays I'd pause, breathless, and wonder at the incredible loveliness of his imagination and the soundness of his reasoning. His emotions were so universal, so widely applicable, and yet at the same time so singular. The rare beauty of his thought and his supreme artistry in expressing it almost stunned me. It seemed as though he could dissect the human mind into parts and lift them one by one to the light and show them to the eyes of the world. It seemed to me he had revealed the mind of man as no one has before or since.

Next I began to read Shaw. If meeting Shakespeare was like a breeze from Heaven, meeting Shaw was like a fresh wind from the sea in March. I delighted in his wit and caustic humor, even if his logic was a bit illogical at times. I soon became devoted to him. It seemed he had an answer for everyone. He may have been what people call an atheist, but I think he was too anxious to make others believe in his atheism for him to really believe in it himself. Perhaps he had an inner belief, or at least an urge to believe, which he concealed beneath an outer pride. I certainly don't know, for his mind was too subtle for me, but reading his plays was as brisk and stimulating an exercise for me as a morning run along the sea strand is for most people.

Sometimes, on nights when I sat in my study at home supposedly reading Caesar or making out problems in geometry or arithmetic, I'd suddenly stop and start thinking of all the girls I could have met, all the girls I could have danced with and perhaps made love to, like Peter and Paddy, my brothers. It wasn't easy, then, to sit in a chair and read, or try to read. Caesar's campaign in Gaul, the History of the Middle Ages, or even Shakespeare. I still had a pain in my mind. I was just twenty years old. I wanted other company besides books. I knew their danger as well as their charm, and I wanted to escape from that danger, to break away from the spell and black magic of constant reading. At these times I didn't care about becoming educated or writing. I wanted to know the joy of climbing a mountain on an early spring morning or of strolling home in the moonlight along rain-washed city streets with a beautiful girl by my side.

I remember one evening when I felt particularly isolated and jealous of Peter and Paddy, who had gone out with their pals. I was left alone, I was sick of reading. For a time I sat morosely, doing nothing. Francis came in for dictation. He sat down, took out his pen, and waited. I knew I had something to say, something to express, but it wouldn't come. I thought and thought, but it was no use, the words were all wrong and twisted. I looked down at my hands, useless as ever. Then, suddenly, I remembered my left foot.

"Get to hell out of here, Francis," I shouted.

Poor Francis looked at me as if he was going to cry.

"Go on," I said. "Out—"

He got up and, looking at me over his shoulder like a frightened rabbit, slipped out of the room. Then I flung myself onto my bed, tore off my left shoe, ripped off my left sock with the other foot, seized a pencil between my first and second left toes, and began to write.

I wrote and wrote, without pause, without consciousness of my surroundings, hour after hour. I felt a different person. I wasn't unhappy any more. I didn't feel frustrated or shut up any more. I was free, I could think, I could live, I could create. . . . Suddenly the door opened and the doctor came in. I stopped, tucked my left foot under me and tried to grin at him, and said something about "a cold evening." He didn't appear to notice anything but sat down by the fire and began to talk about ordinary things. After a while he came round to the subject of the book.

"So you had to call out the old left foot again," he said. I pulled it from under me rather sheepishly. "I wondered," he said, "how long you could stick it. Dictation is not quite enough, is it? Well, I understand. We won't tell Eirene Collis. But don't use it except when you must."

I felt released, at peace. I could be myself sometimes anyway. And if I couldn't know the joy of dancing, I could know the ecstasy of creating.

16

RED ROSES FOR HER

THE BURL IVES concert in Dublin will always remain one of the most exciting days of my life. It all came about in an unusual way. Among Dr. Collis' queer family, of which I am now too a member, is a small Hungarian-Slovak whom the doctor adopted in Belsen. He is a dark-haired, dark-skinned kid with dancing eyes. He was very ill when the doctor found him, and recently the old place in his lung got bad again and he had to have a big operation in the Chest Hospital in London. Burl Ives had met him in Dublin before and taken a great liking to him. So now he used to visit him quite often in the Chest Hospital where he would sing folk songs for the kid and the other men in the ward.

One afternoon Dr. Collis was in London, consulting with Sir Clement Price Thomas about the boy who was now convalescent, having had half his left lung removed. They came into the ward and found a regular concert in full swing. Burl Ives had everybody laughing and singing. Suddenly Dr. Collis got an idea and asked him if he would give a concert in Dublin in aid of cerebral palsy. Burl Ives agreed immediately.

On returning to Dublin, the doctor came out to see me and told me what had happened.

"The idea is," he said, "that Burl Ives will sing and I

shall make an appeal for cerebral palsy. But I think it would be much more to the point if you did."

"Me," I said, "How . . . ?"

"With your foot," he said.

"My foot," I said.

He grinned, "You've finished your first chapter, about the letter A and your mother," he said. "If I were to read them that, they'd know much more about cerebral palsy from the inside than if I were to talk to them for an hour. But you must come along with me and sit beside me so that they'll know it's your work not mine."

I thought a moment. I had visions of sitting before a large audience and seeing hundreds of faces looking up at me, unknown faces, questioning faces with peering eyes, noting my queer movements, my twisting hands and crooked mouth. I hesitated. He put his head slightly on one side. He read my thoughts.

"You can take it?" he said.

"O.K." I said, "I can, of course—"

But I felt scared enough.

Arrangements went ahead at great speed. The Ireland-America Society was induced to sponsor the occasion, and many distinguished people were invited. The Aberdeen Hall in Gresham Hotel, a huge lovely room seating over five hundred people, was taken, tickets were issued, notices were put in the press, interviews were obtained with well-known columnists. The whole city knew about it, but in no quarter more than in our house. All the family said they must come to hear Burl Ives. Mother also said she wanted to hear Dr. Collis read my chapter. But it seemed to me that if the whole family and friends got free tickets they could easily fill the whole hall, and there wouldn't be much left for cerebral palsy! Fierce arguments raged for days. Of course, mother and father had to come. Then Peggy said she was determined to sit beside me. That got her in. Mona and her husband Tom said they'd buy tickets. Tony, Peter, Paddy, Jim, Eamonn, Seàn, Francis, Danny said they wouldn't buy tickets, not to hear me! Lily and Ann didn't get a chance to express their views, but it was assumed that they were coming anyway. Then there was the question of how we were all to get from Crumlin to O'Connell Street in the center of the city on a Sunday afternoon, and how I was to be got into the Gresham Hotel, which has a large open lounge inside the front door always full of people. Mona said, "We better hire a Corus Iompairr Eireann bus."

However, in the end, a friend of the family, Sid Mac-Keogh, who owns an immense American-type taxi, volunteered to bring the Browns in force.

Robbie Collis, the doctor's tall, fair-haired, powerful, medical-student son said he would steer me in through a door at the back of the hotel and get me into my seat before the show started.

The day arrived. All that morning our house looked like a public house on Saturday night with everyone bumping into one another and all talking at the same time. Mother got a loan of a fur coat from a friend and tried it on. "What do I look like?" she asked, taking up different poses as she stood in the center of the kitchen.

There was a hush in the conversation at the table as we turned round to view our model. Nobody spoke. None of us wanted to commit ourselves on such a difficult question. At last Peter picked up his newspaper again and said casually, his eyes intent on the page:

"I see a bear escaped from the zoo last night. . . ."

Mother did not condescened to hear this remark, and, getting out her London hat, put it on in front of the mirror. Mona tried to persuade her to put on some lipstick and powder, but mother said she didn't want to be poisoned.

Father, too, broke out. He had bought a new suit and a funny sort of hat that seemed to be a cross between a trilby and a bowler. He now appeared, looking extremely smart. The hat fitted his head perfectly.

They then started to dress me up in a dinner jacket which they'd got out on hire between them without telling me anything about it. Despite my protests, I was squeezed into it grimly by Peter and Tony. "Have to look proper," they said.

The taxi arrived punctually and we set out like a royal family in a carriage and pair. Only half a dozen of us

could be crammed into it, so the others went by bus:
brothers, sisters, brothers-in-law, sisters-in-law, nephews,
nieces—about a dozen and a half or so, not to mention a
whole retinue of friends and other relatives who followed
after. It was like a regiment on the march when they all
set off down the street together, linking arms.

We drove to Dr. Collis' house where Robbie squeezed
in along with us by either sitting on somebody's knee or
somebody sitting on his, I forget which.

At last we reached the hotel. The others disembarked
at the front entrance first, and then the car drove me
round to the back. I imagined I was quite a heavyweight,
but Robbie Collis just bent down, picked me up in his
arms, and carried me in without even a grunt. The show
hadn't started yet and the curtain hadn't gone up, so I was
put sitting in a chair beside mother, father, Peggy, Tony
and his wife, Sheila. From the other side of the curtain I
could hear the people talking and shuffling as they settled
into their seats. I knew there was a huge crowd in the hall
and that the curtain would rise any second now. I felt
awful. A lot more people had turned up than had had
tickets and many of these were crammed in at the back of
the stage behind us. I looked round and saw that I had
been placed on the right of the stage, the center being left
vacant except for three or four chairs which were now being occupied by the President of the Ireland-American Society, Mr. John Huston, the film producer, and Dr. Collis.
There was a dazzling-looking lady I felt must be a film star
just behind and crowds of people I didn't know.

Then I caught sight of something very remarkable
through the small door at the side of the stage. It was a
man, but all I could see at first was a huge expanse of gold
waistcoat and green trousers. Then the rest of their owner
came into view. I thought I had never seen anything so
enormous and resplendent before. For not only had the
man bulk but he had height, too. He must have stood over
six feet high and weighed over twenty stone. He had a
smiling moonlike face, small eyes, and a pointed beard. He
carried a guitar across one shoulder. He seemed to me

fantastic, like a giant out of a fairy story, amidst the crowd of ordinary mortals. This was Burl Ives.

The next moment the curtain went up and the show was on. I gripped the sides of the chair and tried to hold myself rigid. All I could see was a huge white blur of faces staring up at me. I felt myself go hot and cold in turn. I was conscious of every involuntary movement I made, no matter how slight, and my own awareness of them magnified them into painful conspicuousness. It seemed as if I was alone on the stage with a fierce, bright light beating down on me, as if I was under the lens of a microscope so that not one movement I made could escape detection. I felt I was being watched by a thousand eyes, and I felt the old panic rising within me.

Then Burl Ives began to sing. He had a wonderful, soft, mellow voice with a humorous twist in it, and his style of singing was artful and droll. I just shut my eyes and listened to his singing and half forgot my stage fright.

Soon I was laughing like everyone else as he sang "The Blue-Tailed Fly," "Mr. Frog Went A'Courting," "The House Where Grandmother Dwells." Finally he had everyone singing with him.

There was an old woman who swallowed a fly.
Now I don't know why she swallowed a fly—
Perhaps she'll die. . . .

I found myself singing like everyone else in the hall.

I'd laughed so much that I'd quite forgotten everything else. Then suddenly he stopped and walked off stage. After several encores, he finally withdrew. Then the President of the Ireland-America Society announced that Dr. Collis would address the audience on behalf of the Cerebral Palsy Association.

The doctor got up and went to the microphone. The crowd before him was still in a jovial mood laughing and talking. It wasn't going to be easy to interest them.

He took my manuscript from his pocket and placed it on the stand in front of him.

"I'm not going to make a speech," he said. "I'm not even

going to make an appeal. I'm just going to read you something that will give you an inside view of a person crippled with cerebral palsy. The first chapter of Christy Brown's autobiography here—" he held out his hand toward me—"written with his left foot."

Then he began to read. For the first few minutes there was still a good deal of noise in the audience, people shuffling their feet, and coughing. I saw one man reading a morning paper. Obviously he had come to enjoy a concert, not to be made to listen to a lecture on cripples.

Gradually, however, as the doctor read on, movement and noise ceased; there was silence, complete stillness. I looked down at the faces before me, but now they were no longer just questioning faces with peering eyes, but intent friendly faces full of interest, no longer seeming to look at me, but fixed on the doctor as he went on reading my chapter. They were listening!

I was still tense, still taut as a telegraph wire, sitting on the stage in full view. But after a while I, too, began to listen, and as I did so my tension left me. I forgot my queer hands, twisting and twining in my lap. I forgot my crooked mouth and shaking head. I listened . . . was this true, me, sitting on a stage with mother and father before a huge audience, listening to a description of my own childhood? Had I really written all that stuff? Did all that really come out of my mind? It seemed as if I was dreaming.

I listened. . . . I remembered the day, that December day, when I had first drawn the letter "A" with a bit of yellow chalk in my left foot, with mother kneeling beside me on the wooden kitchen floor, urging me not to give in. . . . I remembered my brothers, the day Tony stripped me behind a bush, put Jim's enormous togs on me, and swung me into the canal, while poor Jim stood by and cried, "He'll drown . . . I tell yer." I remembered the awful day when I found out about myself, the horror I felt, knowing I would be a cripple all my life, and the painting days and the lonely nights in bed, Peter snoring silently in the dark. . . . I remembered Lourdes and the candles flickering before the Grotto . . . and Sheila coming into the Clinic on December mornings, her fair hair scattered by the wind and the rain on her face. . . .

Suddenly I became aware that the doctor had stopped speaking. There was complete silence in the big hall. I saw somebody in the front row crying. I looked aside at mother, sitting upright, her eyes glistening. I looked at father, he was twisting his hat in his hands, he looked at me in a new way. Still there wasn't a sound. Now Dr. Collis walked across the stage, laid his hand on my shoulder and helped me to my feet. Then the cheering broke out. . . . It went on and on and seemed to cover us like waves of the sea.

Suddenly somebody from the audience brought forward a huge bouquet of roses. The doctor stooped and took them. He walked over to where mother was standing. He held up his hand. The cheering stopped.

"I think you will agree," he said to the audience, "that there is only one thing to be done—red roses for Mrs. Brown! For you, Ma'am!" he said, handing the bouquet to mother with a bow. The cheering started again. I could see a group of my brothers way at the back of the hall—Jim, Francis, Paddy, Peter and Seàn—cheering and yelling like hell.

Mother took the bouquet, looking like a Queen Mother, as if she was quite used to roses every day of her life. I thought her face was rather red, but I didn't know if it was the roses or the fur coat. Standing beside her was father, his shoulders drooping and his bald head bent forward. As mother laid the flowers across her arm, I heard her say in a loud whisper out of the corner of her mouth:

"Straighten up, Paddy, can't yer!" Father stiffened but dropped his hat. Peggy picked it up. Then Burl Ives came on again. He began to sing our own Irish folk songs. "She Moved Through the Fair," his own version of "The Spanish Lady."

Now I could relax and enjoy it completely. I was at peace, happy. I lay back in my chair while my old left foot beat time to the rhythm of the tune.

Epilogue

CEREBRAL PALSY IS *a medical term which covers a number of conditions due to brain injury usually occurring during the process of birth or shortly afterwards. The symptoms will depend upon the part of the brain injured. If the higher part of the brain is affected, the child will be stiff or what is called spastic; if the middle part, he will show all sorts of abnormal writhing movements, particularly when he tries to carry out any co-ordinated effort, athetosis; or if the back part of the brain is affected the result will be loss of balance, atoxia. There are other varieties, but these are the main ones conveyed by the general term cerebral palsy.*

As children learn not only through the senses of sight and sound but also through touch and movement, all the cases, of whatever variety, are retarded in their mental development as babies, and it is extremely hard sometimes to ascertain whether they are, in fact, primarily mentally defective due to coincident damage to the thinking center of the brain, or essentially mentally normal but retarded due to failure of normal movement. On the whole, it may be said that the spastics tend often to be genuinely mentally backward and the athetoids (unco-ordinated-movement cases) mentally perfectly normal.

Christy Brown belongs to the athetoid group. He was a bad case and except for his left leg and foot was completely unable to control movement of any kind. The result was that he could not use the muscles of speech or movement and for a long time was unable to make any normal co-ordinated movement or make his speech understood, except to his immediate family, who gradually came to understand his queer grunts and noises as one may a foreign language.

It has only been comparatively recently discovered that these cases can be greatly helped by treatment. Up to a decade ago, cases of cerebral palsy were to be found all over the place in back rooms, a few in orthopedic clinics, or in general out-patient departments, but little was being done for them. Glen Phelps, in Baltimore, and Carlson, himself an athetoid who had managed to become a doctor in America, showed how a completely new approach could benefit these cases. Instead of cutting taut muscles and using splints, the children were taught to use the nerves which still existed undamaged. It was found that in many cases the children could be completely rehabilitated, could in fact be taught to walk and speak almost normally and many, the majority if gotten early enough, could be vastly improved.

The work of rehabilitation and re-education is, however, extremely slow and arduous, requiring much patience of patient and teacher alike. It may be likened to treating a stutterer or learning to write with the left hand. In Southern Ireland we calculate that there are probably about five hundred of these cases of all ages in the population of three million at any one time.

Christy Brown was a particularly severe case of athetosis caused by an abnormal birth in the Rotunda Hospital where "the master" had not expected him to live. He was so "paralyzed" that if it had not been for the tremendous persistence of his extraordinary mother, he would probably have been shut away and utterly imprisoned in a home for mentally defective children and might never have escaped. Due, however, to his mother and the acceptance of him as an ordinary member of the family by his father and all his many brothers and sisters he was able to remain at home, and to learn to read, and write with his left foot.

It was not till he was seventeen, however, that I started the first clinic for cerebral palsy in Ireland, having been initiated into the new forms of treatment by my sister-in-law, Eirene Collis, who had introduced into Europe the methods she had learned from Phelps and others which she had elaborated herself.

At seventeen it is very late to start the treatment of

athetosis, which must commence with learning how to release, for already the patient has got many fixations, both in mind and muscle. Hence, it was by no means an easy job to take on Christy Brown as a patient. My sister-in-law felt that he had put so much into writing and expressing himself with his left foot that if he continued to use it he would fail completely to carry out the various exercises which were the basis of the treatment perscribed for him. Hence he was made at first to give up using his left foot altogether, though as time went on I allowed him to make some use of it when it was the only way he could express himself, and to prevent that was to create a worse tension which would have still more retarded his progress.

He has come on greatly during the last few years: he has learned to sit straight, to stand, to walk with great difficulty across the room and to speak so that the ordinary person can understand him, though he still has to struggle to form many words normally. He is still immensely handicapped as his hands are almost useless, so that he cannot feed himself or dress himself without help. Indeed, I am somewhat concerned as to how he is to continue "to write" as the supply of young bricklayer's apprentices to act as his secretaries cannot last much longer. He is improving all the time, however, and I have hopes that the publication of this work may enable him to obtain an electric typewriter which he could manipulate with one of his hands.

In recent photographs of Christy Brown one sees the look of the boy painting with his left foot. You can see how the muscles of the mouth are drawn in by the athetoid spasm, but the whole gives the impression of one who has mastered himself through hard discipline.

R. C.

THE INCREDIBLE STORY
OF A MAGNIFICENT REBEL
WHO WOULD LIVE FREE...
OR NOT AT ALL!

THE INTERNATIONAL BEST SELLER
NOW A POCKET 📖 BOOK

"A tale of adventure such as few of us could ever imagine,
far less survive."—Book-of-the-Month Club News

▼ AT YOUR BOOKSTORE OR MAIL THE COUPON BELOW ▼